TO SET AT LIBERTY

TO SET AT LIBERTY

Christian Faith and Human Freedom

Delwin Brown

ORBIS BOOKS

Maryknoll, New York 10545

The Catholic Foreign Mission Society of America (Maryknoll) recruits and trains people for overseas missionary service. Through Orbis Books Maryknoll aims to foster the international dialogue that is essential to mission. The books published, however, reflect the opinions of their authors and are not meant to represent the official position of the society.

Manufactured in the United States of America

Biblical quotations are from the Revised Standard Version

Library of Congress Cataloging in Publication Data

Brown, Delwin, 1935-
  To set at liberty.

  Includes bibliographical references and index.
  1. Freedom (Theology) I. Title.
BT810.2.B78 1981   230   80-21783
ISBN 0-88344-501-8 (pbk.)

To Nancy

He opened the book and found the place where it was written,
"The Spirit of the Lord is upon me,
because he has anointed me to preach good news to the poor.
He has sent me to proclaim release to the captives
and recovering of sight to the blind,
to set at liberty those who are oppressed,
to proclaim the acceptable year of the Lord."
                                        —*Luke 4:17b–19*

Contents

Foreword, *by John B. Cobb, Jr.*   xi
Preface   xv

PART ONE
FREEDOM AS A CONTEMPORARY ISSUE

Chapter One
The Question of Freedom: An Historical Sketch   3
Ancient Alternatives   3
The Roman Transition   10
Modern Experiments   12
Freedom: A Post-Modern Possibility   14

Chapter Two
The Nature of Freedom: A Philosophical Perspective   21
Sartre's Existentialism   22
Sartre's Marxism   24
A Whiteheadian Synthesis   28
Elements of Freedom   31

PART TWO
A CHRISTIAN THEOLOGY FOR FREEDOM

Chapter Three
The Lure Toward Freedom: An Understanding of God   43
The Problem of Freedom and God   43
Aseity and Agape   47
The Freedom of God   51
God and Human Freedom Reconsidered   56

Chapter Four
The Denial of Freedom: An Understanding of Sin   64
The Situation of Sin: Anxiety   64
The Forms of Sin: Pride   66
The Forms of Sin: Sensuality   70
The Strategy of Sin: Self-Deception   73
The Objectification of Sin: Original Sin   75
The Consequence of Sin: Death   82

Chapter Five
The Confirmation of Freedom: An Understanding of Christ   88
Jesus as the Gospel of Freedom   88
Jesus as the Gift of Freedom   92
Jesus as the Power for Freedom   98

Chapter Six
The Future of Freedom: An Understanding of Salvation   108
The Abandonment of Hope for History   108
The Recovery of Hope for History   113
The Hope for Freedom in History   121

Index   135

Foreword

The greatest event in twentieth century church history was the Second Vatican Council. The greatest achievement which this event has made possible is the liberation theology and praxis of Latin America. In this event and in this achievement freedom has won a great victory.

The consequences of this victory have been almost as important for Protestants as for Catholics. Indeed they have included the destruction of the great wall that separated these two communities for so long. For a while this seemed to render Catholic thought highly dependent upon the last two centuries of Protestant theological development. But the actual result is that the great initiatives of the global Christian movement are now in the hands of Catholics. Insofar as there is a center for the theology of the Protestant/Orthodox World Council of Churches, that center is constituted by the primarily Catholic theology of liberation.

Sadly, however, we must recognize that while liberation theology advances in the Third World, First World churches are drawing back from their supportive interest. This is equally true of Catholics and Protestants, of Germans and North Americans. Churches in the First World are attending to increasing demands of their more conservative constituencies and seem less and less able to adopt positions that transcend economic and national interests. It seems all too likely that in the eighties a politicized Third World Christianity will confront a First World church concerned for otherworldly salvation and peace of mind and whose political dimension is exhausted by its nostalgia for an older morality and its sanctification of existing structures of power.

Such an eventuality is not inevitable. Christians are not simply victims of fate. Among the many factors responsible for the present drift, one is the failure of First World theologians to respond adequately and appropriately to the challenge of liberation theology. This is not to say that there has been no response. On the contrary, there has been close interconnection between German political theology and Latin American theology, and the seventies saw increasing attention to liberation theologies in the seminaries and church bureaucracies of the United States. But most of the response in English-language contexts was of two types: one, a largely uncritical adulation, and two, a rather condescending dismissal of the central thrust of liberation theology while approving of limited contributions. Neither of these responses could have much effect upon actual church life in this country.

The widely recognized point is that there is a great gap between admiration of the achievements of liberation theology in Latin America and the development of a theology that can function effectively in the middle-class churches of the United States. Even in Latin America, where libera-tion theology allies itself with feelings of national aspiration, it lacks support from middle-class churches. In the United States, where its implications seem to counter national interest as well as class interest, it is unrealistic to expect that many people will be moved to action by direct confrontation with its teachings. A few are radicalized, but these are more likely to be alienated from the churches than to provide effective leader-ship.

What alternatives are there? Three kinds of response are more promis-ing in the United States than direct advocacy of Latin American liberation theology. First, the ideas of liberation theology can be effective in com-munities which experience themselves as oppressed within the United States. For this use, however, black theology is at least equally appropriate, and the need is as much to establish and display the positive relation of black theology and liberation theology as to import Latin American theol-ogy. The Theology in the Americas conferences are already at work here.

Second, hard thinking is needed, stimulated by liberation theology, about the interconnection of our public and private lives in the United States with the total global situation. Such thinking will need to include factors which liberation theologians do not emphasize as well as those they do. It will also have to develop images of a hopeful future for people in our nation which at the same time would not continue to be exploitative and repressive in relation to other peoples. It is important that those who are sensitive to liberation theology will increasingly make their contribu-tions to the large and complex literature about the future of the United States.

Third, there is need for a critical appraisal of the more strictly theologi-cal achievement of liberation theology. Through such an appraisal the results of this theology can be appropriately assimilated into the ongoing theological traditions in the United States. This requires both attention to the central themes of liberation theology and wrestling with the particular doctrines and formulations of liberation theologians. In this way a com-munity of theological discussion can be established and the relevance of Latin American theologies to practice in the dominant North American church can begin to appear through the mediation of North American theologies. The importance of Delwin Brown's book is that it embodies and promotes this third form of response.

Brown's book makes evident how natural it is for North American theologians to share in the themes of liberation theology. Karl Barth astutely observed that when the United States produced its own theology, this should be a theology of freedom. *To Set at Liberty* is just such a theology of freedom.

Brown believes that the Latin Americans have not only struck the right chords in their emphasis of liberation but also that they have made important advances in their discussion of such fundamental topics as the Kingdom of God and its relation to history. He does not believe that they have spoken the last word on these topics or that the appropriate response is to assume that because we are the oppressors rather than the oppressed, we should simply stand aside or let them instruct us. Their discussion includes elements of vagueness we may help to clarify; it raises questions we may help to answer; and it opens up new areas we may help to explore.

Brown undertakes to do all this. But his book is not only a discussion with liberation theology. It is also an independent study of topics of perennial interest. He places the contemporary discussion of freedom in historical perspective, showing the senses in which it is continuous with the Bible and the senses in which it is new. He displays the achievement of Sartre as well as his limitations and shows how the Marxist Sartre could better explain his understanding of the conditioned character of freedom if he overcame his crudely materialist view of nature. He develops original doctrines of sin as the denial of freedom and of Christ as the confirmation of freedom. Everywhere there are analyses and insights that will strike home to many readers.

The author's perspective is deeply shaped by his seminary study with Daniel Day Williams. From him Brown learned his sensitivity to the rich matrix of theological images and concepts. He gained also a profound appreciation of Reinhold Niebuhr combined with dissatisfaction with Niebuhr's dualism and unintended discouragement of efforts to achieve a better world. And he was grasped by the power of Whitehead's vision and conceptuality and the conviction of its fruitfulness for Christian theology.

Because the influence of Whitehead's thought is so strong, *To Set at Liberty* may also be read as an essay in process theology. It contributes to that theological tradition especially in two ways. First, it enriches its doctrinal content. For example, process theology has not sufficiently developed its understanding of sin. To a large extent leading process theologians have simply assumed that this doctrine was adequately and appropriately worked out by Reinhold Niebuhr. Brown's formulations, also, are deeply influenced by Niebuhr, but Brown does not on that account neglect to work out the doctrine. The result is to make explicit just how a basically Niebuhrian doctrine of sin can be modified and expressed in the context of process theology.

Second, Brown opens process theology effectively to dialog and interaction with other traditions, especially that of liberation theology. Once again, few process theologians will find this inappropriate. We remember that our tradition arose at Chicago in the context of commitment to the social gospel. We regret that in the past generation our promotion of concern for the oppressed has been muted. We are grateful to liberation theology for taking up these concerns in so powerful and effective a manner. We see the need of being ourselves transformed by the critical objection to our bourgeois captivity which liberation theologians raise against us. And we are grateful to Brown for guiding us into engagement with the concrete issues that are raised for us in this encounter.

Of course there is much more to be done. North American theologians have been sensitized by the women's movement to a range of issues that has not yet seemed pressing to Latin Americans. We cannot neglect these as we learn from our neighbors to the South. We have been alerted to the responsibility of our Christological formulations for the genocidal behavior of Christian peoples toward Jews. These lessons, too, we must bring to bear in our appropriation of Latin American insights. And it may be that we have thought more about the impact of economic and political policies upon the sustainability of food production than is apparent in the literature of liberation theology. Our task is not to discard what we have already learned in order to absorb the new lessons of the Latin Americans. Our task is to work toward a new understanding of our faith which is sensitive to all this and much more.

Furthermore, one of the most important lessons the Latin Americans have to teach us is that improved understanding by itself will not go far to produce those changes in United States policy, our church life, or personal lifestyles which must occur before our national role ceases to block the movement of political liberation in Latin America and elsewhere. The message of liberation theology is that doctrines developed outside the matrix of practice are likely to have too little effect upon practice. Process theology must learn this lesson too. But meanwhile we can be grateful that Brown has done much to pave the way to partnership between one strand of North American theology and the great movement of Latin American theology.

John B. Cobb, Jr.

Preface

This is an essay on freedom.

The question of freedom in our time is unique to our time. The meaning freedom now has is a distinctively modern meaning, as we shall argue, even through its roots are deep in Western history. Thus, the decision we face regarding freedom's value is a new decision. An essay on freedom cannot "prove" the worth of freedom, but it can clarify the meaning freedom has for us and show what is at issue in our decision about the worth of freedom so conceived. Our initial task is to achieve such clarification.

This is a Christian essay on freedom.

To choose to speak from a Christian standpoint is not to imply that this is the only perspective from which one can speak of and for freedom. It does imply, of course, that the Christian faith is one perspective which can sustain the human search for freedom. But this supposition, even if substantiated, would not provide an adequate basis for our approach apart from another: namely, that the Christian vision of reality remains a fundamental ingredient of the Western sense of value. Whatever the future holds, at the present time the intuitive starting point of most of us in the West, "religious" or not, is dimly but firmly grounded in those sensibilities associated with the traditions of Christianity. If we can show how the power of this perspective enriches our understanding of freedom and supports freedom's increase, then the validity of a liberated existence, from the standpoint of those who share these sensibilities, will have been won. Our analysis of freedom, thus, will be a theology for freedom.

It should be made clear, however, that we do not speak of a peculiarly Christian notion of freedom. To define freedom as being whatever it is that Christianity is thought to provide, e.g., eternal salvation or bondage to Christ, is to betray from the start that freedom which concerns human beings as such. We are speaking of a freedom the meaning of which is not tied to purely Christian presuppositions; we are speaking, in this sense, of a "secular" view of freedom. Our fudamental task, therefore, is to see whether a Christian analysis can provide a basis for, and can strengthen, a secular understanding of freedom and the pursuit of that freedom's realization.

Finally, this is an essay in "process theology."

The process view of the world—as articulated, for example, in the philosophy of Alfred North Whitehead—holds that reality is ultimately constituted by events rather than by substances or enduring things, and that these events are essentially social or interdependent rather than self-contained. In the area of theology this means, among other things, that change and relatedness are introduced into the concept of God. God *is*, for the process viewpoint no less than for traditional theology, but God's being is a mode of social activity even, indeed, as our being is fundamentally a mode of such acitivity.

What else may be said theologically from a process perspective will emerge throughout the book.[1] It must be stressed, however, that our analysis seeks to provide a *Christian* understanding of freedom's worth. The conceptual categories employed in this analysis are those of process philosophy, but our dependence upon these categories is far from decisive. Whitehead himself insisted upon the tentative and temporary adequacy of his philosophical system.[2] Surely the theologian as a Whiteheadian, to say nothing of the theologian as a Christian, should do likewise. Thus, in its fundamental commitment, this is a Christian theology for freedom.

Marjorie Suchocki, Russell Pregeant, John B. Cobb, Jr., and Ignacio Castuera read the entire manuscript and suggested a number of changes that strengthened the book substantially. I am particularly indebted to them. Others read portions of the manuscript and made important suggestions. These include: Adelle Allen, Hendrikus Boers, Rita Brock, Bettie Ann Doebler, Lewis Ford, David Griffin, Frederick Herzog, Bernard Lee, Lori Krafte, and Willard Reed, as well as members of our department—James Foard, Joel Gereboff, Sam Gill, Richard Martin, Rosemary Rader, and Richard Wentz—whose discussion of parts of the material benefited me. I sincerely thank all of these people, and free them of responsibility for the ways their contributions were put to use.

To Nancy, my wife, and to our daughters, Terri, Kimberli, and Kristen, I am deeply and happily indebted, for their help in this undertaking and for all those other sacred things.

Notes

1. Authors of books in Christian theology utilizing a Whiteheadian process conceptuality include William A. Beardslee, John B. Cobb, Jr., David R. Griffin, Bernard Lee, S.M., Bernard Meland, Robert B. Mellert, Schubert M. Ogden, Norman Pittenger, Paul R. Sponheim, Daniel Day Williams, and Clark Williamson.

2. Alfred North Whitehead, *Process and Reality* (New York: Macmillan Company, 1929), pp. x, 48–50, 127f.

TO SET AT LIBERTY

PART ONE

Freedom as a Contemporary Issue

Chapter One

The Question of Freedom: An Historical Sketch

Talk of freedom pervades modern discussion at virtually every point of importance. It is prominent in our considerations of institutional structures like politics and religion. It is central to our thinking about more intimate relationships such as marriage, morality, and the educational experience. It is almost omnipresent.

The pervasiveness of talk about freedom may lead us to suppose that we are here having to do with a matter of perennial human concern. That supposition is false. Since the middle of the nineteenth century the question of freedom has emerged in a unique fashion. It confronts us differently from the way in which it was posed for previous generations. It confronts us differently from the way in which other issues are posed for us today. Freedom is uniquely our problem—that is the claim this chapter endeavors to clarify and to sustain.

To view freedom as being our problem in a special sense is not to deny its firm rootage in the past. On the contrary, only by understanding something of its history do we understand the uniqueness of the problem before us. The present chapter sketches that history. It does not provide a complete account of ideas of freedom in the West. Rather, it traces the history of certain crucial elements of the question of freedom as that question emerges in its distinctively modern form. In this way we shall see how and why freedom has become the central problem for our modern self-understanding, individually and corporately.[1]

Ancient Alternatives

The origin of freedom and indeed of modern culture itself is commonly located in what Karl Jaspers has called the Axial Period, ranging roughly from 800 to 200 B.C.[2] During this period the basic schools of Chinese philosophy came into being, in India Buddhism arose and the Upanishadic literature of Hinduism was produced, the prophets appeared in Israel, and Greece gave birth to philosophy, tragedy, the epic, history, and much of Western art. In this six-hundred-year span there developed the traditions and conceptualities from which we today live and seek to understand ourselves.

There were some intimations of freedom before the Axial Period. The

3

word itself appears in Sumerian records dating from the twenty-fourth century, and the Sumerians give evidence of a fleeting notion of individual autonomy. The upper classes of the Old and Middle Egyptian Kingdoms exhibited what we might call confident spontaneity from time to time, a form of creativity perhaps. In the Later Kingdoms (about 1600–1000 B.C.) there arose an Egyptian middle class that enjoyed some economic independence. More significantly, Akhnaton, who reigned around the middle of the fourteenth century, instituted sweeping social and economic reforms, and he suggested the interesting idea that God "fashions himself." For several reasons, however, these varied antecedents of many concepts of freedom, partial as they must have been, were all shortlived. They did little to alter human self-understanding toward a sense of human freedom. In fact, there is no evidence of a self-understanding at all, as far as we can tell. Pre-Axial peoples generally were unawakened to freedom; hence they were unawakened to their unfreedom. Or, at the very least, no such insights embedded themselves in individual and corporate structures strongly enough to endure perceptibly.

There is one known exception to the above generalization; it is only a partial one, but terribly intriguing. This exception is the Minoan civilization that flourished on the island of Crete from about 2500 to 1200 B.C. The first evidence that Minoa confronts us with something new is apparent in its art, as compared to that of Egypt. The art of ancient Egypt evokes in us a sense of what is timeless and abstract; what is painted, sculpted, and carved in relief are ideal types, devoid of individuality and devoid of the intensity of momentary experience. Minoan art jolts us by its contrast. The animated, spontaneous figures, the fluid forms and undulating lines of Minoan pottery, toreador frescoes, and snake-goddess statuary reveal an apparently unprecedented zest, playfulness, and graceful warmth of human emotion. For various reasons—among them, probably, a high living standard based on trade and commerce, the relative ease of life, and a generally flexible monarchy—something new seems to have been added to the conception of life. It was a sense of the worth of the individual moment. That was still not a sense of individuality, probably, but the locus of reality had moved from the abstract to the concrete, from the timeless to the individual moment. And that was a step toward a conception of freedom.

We do not know the precise impact of Minoan sensibilities upon the Greeks, whose Axial achievements are so fundamental to us. The distance from Crete to the Greek mainland is slight, but the five or six hundred years between the Minoans and the Hellenes is an obscure period. Almost certainly there was some indebtedness. In any case, the Greek spirit, when it finally emerged, exhibited important strains of "Minoan" zest and spontaneity. It also had its "Egyptian" side, however. Indeed, the Greek achievement is far too complex to attempt an adequate treatment here.

Fortunately, it is well enough known to most readers that a broad summary, highlighting only that which is relevant to the thesis of this chapter, will be sufficient. After that we shall give similar attention to the Hebrews, whose perspective constitutes the other main source of our present situation with regard to the question of freedom.

The Greek outlook had two foci. One was an understanding of the self, the other a view of the cosmos. With respect to its conception of selfhood, this outlook centered upon what we might call "intuitive reason." We will find this conjunction of terms difficult to understand. How can anything be both intuitive and rational? Our perplexity is due in part to our narrower idea of reason as being something like the logical calculation of the individual mind. The Greeks had a different notion. They thought of reason as the structure of the cosmos embedded also in the human mind. To speak of humans as being rational, then, was most fundamentally to say that they are essentially in union with the ultimate structure of things. Many qualifications should be added to this statement, of course, but none of them requires that there be an incompatibility between reason, so viewed, and intuition or feeling. At least not in principle. In practice, however, the Greeks did find reason and intuition to be difficult bedfellows. Their conjunction in the Greek experience was as much aspiration as reality.

Recognition of the intuitive dimension of selfhood is the clearest suggestion of a Greek indebtedness to the Minoans. Yet already in its earliest Greek formulation, that of Homer, this deeply emotional dynamic is more profound, more attuned to life's sadnesses than we can justifiably attribute to the people of King Minos. And it has a grander, more heroic cast. The same ethos that tells the movingly sad story of Demeter's loss of Persephone tells too of Odysseus's often painful, often tearful (Greek heros could cry!) but always heroic striving for home. We begin to get a sense of human life as a heart-led adventure, portrayed always, though, with full awareness of the pain and danger of such assertiveness. Freedom, if we may call it that in these vague Homeric notions, is not experienced as an altogether happy thing.

The intuitive element, and its problems, comes to full expression in the mythical figure of Bacchus or Dionysus. In his play *The Bacchae*, Euripides contends that one who denies Bacchus (feeling) is soon consumed by him—"uncontrolled the unbeliever goes." The ideal conveyed in the play, however, is that of a balance of feeling and order. This ideal is expressed superbly in Greek art and architecture. The Parthenon is an example. The Parthenon is not the geometrically perfect structure it seems to be; in fact, its columns are swelled at their centers and its angles slightly skewed to give the appearance of strict proportion. The Parthenon is order, reason, qualified by the rightful demands of feeling. But it is also feeling ordered by reason. Even in Plato's philosophical synthesis of the Greek experience, where the god of reason and order, Apollo, threatens to dominate, it is still a *synthesis* that Plato seeks to achieve, a blending of the rational and the intuitive. In Books VI and VII of the *Republic,* where Plato traces reason's meticulous rise to knowledge, he has Socrates describe reason's consummate union with the Forms as a mystical union, an intuition. Yet it is *reason's* intuition. True self-hood, in this view, is not a combination of distinct faculties, the rational and the intuitive; it is their unity—albeit, perhaps, a unity never fully achieved.

The other focus of the Greek outlook, we said earlier, was a view of the cosmos. Here the ancient Egyptian preference for the eternal comes to the fore. It it expressed by the Greeks in their concept of Moira. Moira is the structure of order at the heart of the universe. At first, in Homer, Moira seems to have been a vague anticipation of natural necessity, a principle explaining why things happen as they do. In this sense Moira has the connotation of fate. But later Hesiod humanizes Moira, so to speak, rendering it as a principle of order that has human well-being as its purpose. "When she comes at length to the end of the race," he tells us, "Justice beats Outrage."

Because of Hesiod's transmutation of Moira, the abstract principle that in an Egyptian context seems to have worked against the development of individuality had an opposite consequence. Hesiod's introduction of a *moral* order created a cleavage between "what is" and "what ought to be" within which the individual could maneuver. Beyond the real was an ideal toward which one could strive. In this way fate, conceived as the moral structure of things, loosened up the universe, creating thereby an arena for human agency.

Human latitude, however, was not extensive. In the final analysis Moira denoted the ultimate limit of things. These limits bound the gods no less than humans. Consequently, the good, the true, and the beautiful were grounded in the nature of reality itself. Thus the appropriate human stance was understanding; it was to grasp rationally and to obey the norms that were objectively given. The chief moral danger was that a person might, through ignorance, breach the limits appropriate to his or her life. Conscious moral rebellion was not a problem. Indeed, *moral* rebellion was inconceivable since the cosmic order against which one might rebel was precisely the order that defined what is moral. As the story of Oedipus illustrates, and as Socrates says, sin is rooted in ignorance, not in the will.

The strong sense of an objective cosmic order entailed a form of life that was contemplative and in that sense passive rather than active. For the Greeks, Hanna Arendt says, the eternal cosmic order "discloses itself to mortal eyes only when all human movements and activities are at perfect rest."[3] This statement could be misleading. The Greeks were often vigorously and systematically curious about the world. They were discoverers. But that is the point behind Arendt's claim: they were discoverers, not creators in the deepest sense.[4] They sought to find the already established cosmic order and to transpose that order into physical and conceptual modes. They did not attempt—it could not have occurred to them to attempt—to bring into being that which was not already there. They did not seek to create the good, true, and beautiful; they sought to find and reflect it.

Another result of this strong sense of cosmic order was the muting of a consciousness of individuality. Indeed, as Herbert J. Muller tells us, there was no word in the Greek lexicon for "individual," "ego," and "self," and there was no clear delineation of the rights of the individual in distinction from those of the state and class.[5] Socrates, often cited as the first manifestation of an autonomous individual conscience, in fact subsumed individual rights to those of the state. Antigone, in the play by Sophocles, does quarrel with the human law, but she does so in the name of higher, "unwritten laws, eternal in the heavens." She does not contend with God. But this conviction of a cosmic moral order, reflected in the structure of the self to which the self must be subservient, produced a sense of the individual's oneness with the nature of things. Where this conviction dominated, one could be painfully alienated from neighbor and from state, but one could not be alienated from that which is ultimately real and that which, ultimately, would prevail.

Perhaps the supreme expression of the Greek understanding of self and world appeared in Stoicism, during the Hellenistic period. Earlier, during the classical era, the self had been viewed, initially at least, in relation to the city-state, the *polis*. Freedom thus was political freedom, independence in the sense of not being a slave; it was membership in the privileged, self-determining class freed of foreign domination and the necessity of physical drudgery. But then the Hellenistic world experienced the crumbling of those political and social structures to which freedom had been related. The Stoic response was to ground the self in a more durable structure, namely, in the Reason or Logos that constitutes the orderly foundation of the cosmos. The inner, rational self was said to be essentially at one with *this* structure, universal and unchanging. Hence, Stoic freedom was an even more fundamental independence than that of the classical period; it was freedom from social institutions and norms, whatever they might be, as well as freedom from bondage to the claims of the physical body. For Stoicism, the self is free when it actualizes its essential independence of all things, *except* the objective, cosmic law. The self's freedom is to be found precisely in its *subjection* to the law of the universe.[6] This is not quite the external constraint it seems to be, however; because the individual reason is essentially at one with the cosmic Reason, bondage to Reason is also bondage to oneself. Nevertheless, freedom does not constitute the cosmic Logos as such and therefore neither does freedom characterize the inner self. Freedom is a type of relationship, it is the self's independence of temporal affairs. But there is no sense in which the self "in itself" *is* freedom.

We turn now to the Hebraic conception of life. Like that of the Greeks, it had two foci, one centering upon the notion of the self and the other on the cosmos. If we propose to begin with the Hebrew notion of the self, however, we are led immediately to their understanding of the world and, specifically, to their view of God. This is because in the Hebrew view, as it has been determinative for Western history, human nature reflects the nature of God—"Let us make man in our image, after our likeness." Hence to understand ourselves aright, on this view, we must first know something about God.

Basic to the Hebraic conception of God is the claim that God is creator. Initially, this claim tells us about God rather than about the world. It emerged, apparently, in the process of defending the supremacy of the Hebrew God over other deities, becoming explicit finally in the eventual triumph of monotheism. Its point is to assert God's unique suprem- acy, or autonomy, no less than to affirm God's rule over the world, God's lordship. In this respect the early idea of divine autonomy already drives toward the later, peculiarly difficult belief that God is *a se*—that God "comes from himself," as Christians were to express it. The total suprem- acy of the one God could be preserved in no other way, it seemed, than by claiming that the divine nature depends on nothing at all outside of itself, especially for its existence. The doctrine that the world is created *ex nihilo*—out of nothing—would appear to be a corollary notion (even though it is not explicit in the Hebrew accounts of creation in Genesis). If one assumes (as did the Hebrews, implicitly, and later the Christians) that the world was not "composed" of the divine nature, of what could it be made? The natural answer, that it is made of some non-divine stuff, was unacceptable to later Jewish and Christian theologians since it entailed that God's creative power would then be restricted by the limitations inherent in that finite material. Hence it would seem necessary to say that God made the world out of nothing. In sum, both doctrines—that God is *a se* and that creation is *ex nihilo*—only attempt to spell out what is already ingredient in the early idea of God's autonomy.

One immediate result of this approach is to make the divine will central to the nature of things. The true, good, and beautiful—to use the Greek ideals—are what they are, not of necessity, but only because God wills them to be so. This means that they are contingent—they could have been otherwise, and, presumably, they could even yet be other than they are. After all, the mind of God is sometimes changed in the Hebrew Bible. We shall see later how this allows for the growth of a sense of individuality. For now it is sufficient to note that all things are traced back to a personal will, not to an impersonal and changeless order, yielding the prospect of a more open, "flexible" universe.

A second result of the Hebrew understanding of God is the emergence of a distinctive concept of the self's freedom and creativity. These ideas of freedom and creativity are not necessarily the same. Neither are they, together or separate, free of perplexities. Even so, the concept of a being who somehow is the creative source of its own existence and who brings a world of structure and value into being out of nothing is a tantalizing concept. And it would seem to be unique. It is doubtful that we have a direct intuition of anything like so radical a moment of creativity in human experience. We have lately been tempted to think of ourselves on the order of this model, and this experiment has, for the most part, been self-consciously secular rather than religious. In fact, however, the source of such thinking is here in the Hebrew idea of God.

If, historically, we have come to project upon the self the creative freedom attributed to the Hebrew God, the way for this development was anticipated by the Hebraic claim that human nature mirrors or images divine nature. The concept of the human self as a creator receives interesting elaboration in Genesis 2. Here God brings all living creatures before Adam "to see what he would call them." To name something, in the Hebrew view, is to give that thing its essence, to order it, to give it a place in the nature of things. Adam's task, then, was not that of reduplicating on earth some form of order that resides originally in heaven. Adam was to create an order, a system of meanings, out of nothing, so to speak. Genesis 2 suggests that the radical creativity attributed to God is also somehow to be mirrored in the human self. "To exist, humanly, is to name the world."[7]

The doctrine of a creative self, however, was not easy to assert within the confines of the Hebraic form of life. How can genuine human creativity be manifested in the light of divine creativity? How can the human will be significantly effective if the divine will has already been exercised? Probably the narratives cited above come relatively late in Israel's development. Already the priority of the divine will had led, inevitably one would think, to the rise of Jewish legalism. What God had freely chosen was transmuted into binding Law. Richard Rubenstein has recently mounted a valuable defense of legalism, arguing that it is essentially a system whereby the individual-in-community may reconcile himself or herself to the necessary rhythms of life.[8] His point is insightful, but it does not deny that legalism's tendency can be to stultify creativity, to cause doubt that Adam really names the animals. Of course freedom remains under a legalism. It is restricted in its function, however, to accepting or rejecting the divinely prescribed order of things. And as the notion of judgment and eternal punishment developed to buttress the divine demands, the reality of human freedom moved toward mere abstraction.

Yet we must see that freedom never became simply an abstraction in this tradition. This is partly attested to by the covenantal literature in which obedience is interpreted as a loving, autonomous action, against all the contrary feelings that must have been experienced. Dwelling in the tension between the divine law and human freedom—a tension often obscured by later Christian reductions of freedom to the law (of Christ)—produced a distinctive genre of searching self-reflection. The depth of anguish, and joy, expressed in the cry, "I love thy Law, oh Lord" must surely be lost upon those of us who do not dwell in this particular tension, even if we have others of our own to endure. In any case, here the sense of oneself as an individual could emerge. Instead of the impersonal domination of a cosmic necessity, as in Greek thought, we have here the personal dominance—at once loving and awesome—of one Will over other wills. The finite will, being called to respond, comes to view itself as being *capable* of response. It is a response for which the self is responsible, an action that is in some important measure not reducible to antecedent circumstance. This brings us to an important point: conceivably, the response could be positive *or* negative. However difficult it may have been at the level of feeling to respond negatively to the divine will, it was possible to do so.

Indeed, the strongest evidence that the Hebraic perspective, in spite of the dominance of legalism, nurtured a distinctive notion of the human self comes in its fostering of *moral* rebellion against God. It appears subtly in the tentative protestations of a Moses or a Jeremiah against God's will for their lives. The book of Job, however, portrays it best. Job refuses to acquiesce to God's will because he thinks *God* is wrong. He swears to defend himself against God's judgment, even without the hope of success and facing certain death. He even demands that God answer to him! The fact that in the end Job yields to God cannot gainsay the fact that we have here—wavering and unsure, but real—a form of human rebellion against God that is distinctive. Job claims to be right although he cannot rest his case on some higher standard than God, such as Moira or the "unwritten law" in Antigone. The contrast with Antigone speaks for itself. Job's rebellion comes from himself. He "names" what is right, contradicting God, and insists that his naming be considered on a par with that of God. Of course Job is a Jewish heretic, but he is a *Jewish* heretic. Only where moral norms are grounded contingently as in the will of the Hebrew God, and only where the human self is fundamentally a will that may also in some measure be said to "name the animals," only here could a Job appear.

The central point, however, is not the moral rebellion of Job, but the idea of the self that made such rebellion even conceivable. If the Greeks thought that our distinctive humanity resides in our rational functioning, or, ideally, in the union of intuition and reason, the Hebrews viewed the matter in volitional terms. Human distinctiveness lies in the act of deciding. Not "know thyself" but "choose you this day" best expresses the Hebrew spirit.

The Roman Transition

We have been examining those resources in the ancient world from which the history of Western self-understanding has developed. It has been impossible to speak more than vaguely of freedom. The word was used, to be sure, but in so many contexts and with so many meanings that an identification of precise standpoints is difficult. More importantly, it is unnecessary. The search for self-understanding was not focused on freedom. Freedom was a peripheral issue, for the most part, and even when it moved momentarily toward the center it was negative in conception (the absence of unwanted constraint) and instrumental in character (a means to some greater end).

Coming out of the ancient world the pursuit of self-understanding took three forms. We have identified only two, the volitional path of the Hebrews and the rational-intuitive alternative of the Greeks. But as already intimated, and as Aristotle's philosophy makes clear, reason and intuition were easily separated during the period of Greek decline. Therefore, subsequent history can readily be seen as the story of the volitional, the rational, and the intuitive conceptions of selfhood, alone and in interaction, enduring in various guises up to the modern period. We can trace this development only in the broadest strokes.

After Plato and Aristotle, the tradition of reason moved through Stoicism into the development of the great system of Roman law. We have already noticed the tendency of the Hebrew view of human nature toward legalism. By the first century this tendency had clearly prevailed in Judaism. Soon after its inception, Christianity, too, moved into legalistic patterns. Together, Judeo-Christian forms of legalism and the Roman legal system worked in tandem to create the social and politico-ecclesiastical structures of the entire medieval period. In this way rationalism became subservient to a variant of the volitional alternative, namely to legalism. The power of reason remained, of course. Eventually its "legal" expression became incorporated, through Neoplatonism, in the concept of the Great Chain of Being, the idea of the hierarchical organization of reality from God, down through persons in their assigned social orders, to the physical universe. But reason's function in this respect was primarily passive; it articulated the established cosmic order. Not until the late Middle Ages did reason emerge again in the active role of the discoverer of truth.

One form of the intuitive alternative was the appropriation of the old epic tradition. Here Virgil's *Aenead*, from about 20 B.C., comes to mind. Virgil was partly a conduit through which the Stoic ideal of brotherhood found imperfect form in Roman law. But, in addition, through the figure of Aeneas, Virgil transmitted the ancient notion of the epic hero true to, if not in charge of, his own destiny. In this way the *Aenead* provided subsequent generations with a *this-worldly* intuitive model, a hero bound by his heart to the performance of his earthly duty. Time and again this model reappeared through the Middle Ages in imaginative allegories of love, war, and duty, showing clearly that a sense of adventure survived amidst legalistic patterns of order.

The other form of the intuitive conception of selfhood was Neoplatonism, a version of Platonism in which a disembodied Bacchus triumphs over Apollo. Its otherworldliness and suspicion of reason profoundly influenced Augustine, whose own synthesis of Judeo-Christian and Greco-Roman sensibilities wrote a large share of subsequent Roman history. The result was that a disembodied spirituality and unrationalism characterized much of medieval culture. But not all. The later rise of the secular codes of courtly love and, inside the Church, the cult of the Virgin probably represent the culmination of a strong tradition *throughout* the medieval period that held together the spiritual and the more plainly sensual expressions of the intuitive side of human experience.

The period from the birth of Christianity through the Middle Ages is one of enormous complexity. The alternatives derived from the past, infinitely more complex than we have described them, were being forced into the funnel of a single history, to which was added the cultural infusions from Byzantium, Islamic civilization, and the Celto-Germanic peoples. The action and reaction of these partially conflicting ideas and modes of life was so tumultuous and intricate that we may wonder whether a divine mind could fathom their interrelationships. One generalization does seem possible from our perspective: Until the late Middle Ages, it was legalism and feeling that most profoundly characterized medieval life. Structure and spontaneity lived together, but they were seldom in harmony and never in unity. Medieval culture gave rise to no single, synthetic view of selfhood prior to the thirteenth century. And when finally one was formulated in the work of Thomas Aquinas, it was dominated by reason, not by will or intuition.

Modern Experiments

Thomas Aquinas is commonly viewed as the culmination of the Middle Ages. In terms of his synthesis of its varied components, certainly, this view is correct. With respect to the centrality of reason in his conception of the self and the world, however, Thomas can also be seen as heralding the appearance of modernity, especially when we recall that that modernity sought first to be a "renaissance" of the classical outlook. Following Aristotle, Thomas subordinated the realms of feeling and of willing to the rational faculty (even though the latter was incorporated within reason, thus making it "higher" than feeling). And following Aristotle, as modified by Christian faith, Thomas placed this self within a vast, interrelated teleological universe, ordered and sustained by a beneficent deity. God's will was the cosmic reason to which human reasoning was subservient.

The primarily rational conception of selfhood that we find in Aquinas was continued by those who dominated Western thought from the Renaissance beginning in the fifteenth century through the Enlightenment in the eighteenth. Whereas Thomas had correlated reasoning with the dictates of the medieval tradition, however, the modern rationalists tried in varying ways, and with differing degrees of success, to tie reason to "the facts." Petrarch's ascent of Mt. Ventoux about 1330, solely "to see its conspicuous height," symbolizes reason's descent into the world of observable reality. It led explorers to seek new routes to the Indies, painters to a consideration of the problems of perspective, writers to a greater realism, and musicians eventually to the strongly ordered music of the classical period. It also gave birth to modern science. Leonardo da Vinci, Francis Bacon, Kepler, Galileo, and the incomparable Newton were its midwives, and the philosopher Descartes was its godfather.

The history of this version of the rational conception of selfhood— reason held close to experience—runs on from Descartes, through the British empiricists to its apparent demise in Hume's skepticism, to its attempted resurrection in the philosophy of Immanuel Kant. In his essay "What is Enlightenment?" Kant had urged his readers to "dare to know" meaning "dare to use your reason," and Kant's philosophy was his extraordinary effort to show that such an injunction was reasonable. His hopes were high. The enlightenment of the masses, he said, is "almost inevitable." Kant was verbalizing a general optimism even more strongly expressed by others, especially in France. "By reasoning and by fact," the Marquis de Condorcet promised, "the progress of human perfectibility . . . can proceed at a pace more or less rapid, but it will never go backward." Trusting in "reason" and "facts," people began to talk about the coming utopia. Nature, including human nature and society, was thought to be governed by principles that reason could discover. Once discovered, these principles could be used to eliminate the defects of individuals and society.

Toward the end of the eighteenth century, the Enlightenment confidence in reason began to wane. It was not refuted by logic; it seemed less and less to fit the realities of life. Reason failed to produce, and the orderly universe it sought failed to inspire. The heady cataclysm called the French Revolution marks as well as anything this change of sensibilities (even if, ironically, its very possibility was due to the Enlightenment's hopefulness). Rather dramatically, the long series of experiments with the rational conception of selfhood, which had stretched over four or five centuries, was replaced by another. This new experiment focused on the intuition, and it was called Romanticism. "I am certain of nothing," John Keats wrote, "but the holiness of the heart's affections." And Wordsworth said:

> One impulse from a vernal wood
> May teach you more of man,
> Of moral evil and of good,
> Than all the sages can.

Likewise in music and the visual arts, there was a concentration upon the unspeakable depths and the mystery of things. Confusion and variety, not order and unity, were seen to be fundamental to the universe. Such a universe could not be explained, it could only be understood—with the heart.

It is important to note that Romanticism, no less than the Rationalism it had supplanted, believed that Something was there to be understood. There is, Romanticism assumed, an Ultimate Truth which is accessible to human inquiry. To be sure, Romanticism replaced Kant's "dare to reason" with its own "dare to feel"—believing, as Blake put it, that "the affections gently lead us on." Still, both Romanticism and Rationalism believed that there was some place where the searching self, following its mind or its heart, could *find* Truth. Neither needed to "name the animals." For both, twin heirs that they were to the classical outlook, life was discovery, not creation in the Hebraic sense of that term. And particularly in that nineteenth-century blend of Rationalism and Romanticism which we call "Victorianism," there was little urge to create. The heavy sense of destiny in its novels, like the firm structures of its social organization, reveals the Victorian's great trust in the givenness of truth, goodness, and (such as it was) beauty. The Victorian period was the last, and the least interesting, classical period.

If Romanticism is not dead today, neither does it show signs of being very durable. Perhaps its ultimate fallacy is already revealed in Thomas Mann's "Death in Venice." The romantic Gustave Aschenbach swoons on the shore of a southern sea, watching the god of beauty play in the waves, never able to approach the god, never able even to speak his name; yet also never able to arise and go, although he knows well that his intoxicated fascination leads to "the bottomless pit" of his own dissolution.

In view of the history we have traced, one might reasonably conclude that our modern experiments with the rational and the intuitive views of selfhood have failed. That is not to say that they are wholly wrong, that reason and feeling have no place in a proper understanding of being human. It is to suggest that they fail to provide the most fundamental answer to the question, what does it mean to be human? We no longer find it adequate to think of ourselves primarily in terms of our reason or primarily in terms of our feeling. If this is true, we may be prepared to re-examine the third alternative, offered in the Hebraic conception of life, which understands being human primarily in terms of choosing, of volition. This option, however, does not emerge as a neat, readily-usable answer. As we shall see, in the way it has been posed for us today, it is so radical that, at most, it appears as a question, not an answer. In fact, the radical manner of its articulation makes one wonder whether *any* answer is possible. But, as we shall also see, the very radicality of this articulation suggests in the fullest degree what it might mean to say that human beings are free.

Freedom: A Post-Modern Possibility?

In summarizing our discussion to this point, we may say that the alternatives for Western self-understanding seem to be threefold. Each of them includes a conception of the self and the world. Two of these alternatives derived from ancient Greece. Their "self" components, originally held together, view being human in terms of "being rational" and "being intuitive." In their conceptions of the world, they agree that the cosmos is a harmonious whole, bound by a principle that holds things together, explains things, and moves them forward. This principle of things is not alien to human beings; we inhabit it and in it we find meaning. Neither is it unknowable. The human task, in fact, is to discover this Truth of things and to place oneself under it. Freedom was not of the essence of these understandings of being human, together or apart. As much as freedom was prized by the Greeks, and as important as the Greeks are for the Western affirmation of freedom's worth, freedom was to them instrumental in character (the means to another end) and negative in conception (the absence of unwanted restrictions).

The third alternative for Western self-understanding was worked out implicitly in Hebrew experience. The Hebraic notion of selfhood centered upon activity, not on passive understanding. It was not activity in the sense of mere performance, which characterizes animals as much as human beings. It was action rooted in choice, in decision. The corresponding Hebrew view of the world affirmed a cosmic structure, an order, a meaning, as did that of the Greeks. But in the Hebrew view the cosmic order was grounded in the will of a personal God. *That* this order is, and *what* it is, are products of God's decision. The concept of freedom was crucial to the Hebrew alternative, albeit primarily as related to its conception of deity. God is free in the sense of being the creative source of meaning and order. Nevertheless, an air of freedom infected also the Hebraic conception of human selfhood, in its emphasis upon decision and action and in its claim that human nature mirrors or images God's nature, extending even to the occasional suggestion that human beings, like God, give structure and significance to the created world. But for the most part human freedom in the radical, positive sense remained an abstraction, an unactualized possibility, held in check by the pre-eminence of God's freedom.

These three alternatives opposed and supplemented each other from the ancient world through the medieval period. The Renaissance tried to revive the classical alternatives. Perhaps briefly, in fifteenth-century Florence, reason and intuition were united, but if so they very soon parted and moved to their respective culminations. The modern experiment with reason led to the Enlightenment. The modern experiment with intuition led to Romanticism. The questionableness, though not the death, of each is now history—our history. Equally a part of our history is the "renaissance" of the third option, derived from Hebraic sensibilities, to which we now turn.

Understandably, Western history is replete with traces of the Hebraic notion of selfhood. This is true even with reference to the radical doctrine that Adam "names the animals." Augustine, for example, writes: "The soul was not . . . given all that it had the power to become . . . [It has received] . . . the power with the aid of the Creator to cultivate itself . . . to attain what [it] did not have. . . ."⁹ Augustine is reflecting the notion that the self in some measure decides its own nature and meaning, although his affirmation is carefully balanced (and, ultimately, almost obscured) by a recognition of divine providence. A similar conception of selfhood, more evenly balanced, appears in Pico della Mirandola's fifteenth-century "Oration on the Dignity of Man." God created Adam, Pico tells us, and then addressed him thus:

> "Neither an established place, nor a form belonging to you alone, nor any special function have We given to you, O Adam, and for this reason, that *you may have and possess,* according to your own desire and judgment, *whatever place, whatever form, and whatever functions you shall desire.* The nature of other creatures, which has been determined, is confined within the bounds pre-scribed by Us. *You, who are confined by no limits, shall determine for yourself your own nature,* in accordance with your own free will, in whose hand I have placed you. I have set you at the center of the world, so that from there you may more easily survey whatever is in the world. We have made you neither heavenly nor earthly, neither mortal nor immortal, so that, more freely and more honorably the molder and maker of yourself, *you may fashion yourself in whatever form you shall prefer.* . . ."
>
> O sublime generosity of God the Father! [Pico continues] O highest and most wonderful felicity of man! *To him it was granted to have what he chooses, to be what he wills.*¹⁰

The idea that humanity is the source of order and meaning, including human meaning, is expressed with increasing clarity and force through-out the modern period until its fullest expression in the nineteenth century. Hegel's philosophy makes the point: "Spirit," Hegel writes in reference to human spirit, "is only what it makes itself become."¹¹ The point is made even more powerfully, though still not in its purest form, in Goethe's *Faust.* Like Aschenbach, in Thomas Mann's story mentioned earlier, Faust despairs of reason

> Torn is the subtle thread of thought,
> I loath the knowledge I once sought.

and turns to feeling

> In sensuality's abysmal land
> Let our passions drink their fill!
> In magic veils, not pierced by skill,
> Let every wonder be at hand!¹²

But the chaotic futility of Romanticism is unveiled in Part I of the drama, both by its form (or formlessness) and its content. So, in Part II, Faust seeks another path to salvation. Although it is not wholly devoid of reason and feeling, Faust's salvation comes in his *willing* to create his own world.

> Green are the meadows, fertile; and in mirth
> Both men and herds live on this newest earth,
> Settled along the edges of a hill
> That has been raised by bold men's zealous will.[13]

Goethe's vision is far from simplistic or naive. He makes altogether clear the anguish, even the cruelty, that can accompany such a posture. He bares, too, the question of its futility. Goethe exalts freedom:

> This is the highest wisdom that I own,
> The best that mankind ever knew:
> Freedom and life are earned by those alone
> Who conquer them each day anew.[14]

Then, only a few lines later he allows the question of its significance to come forward:

> Why have eternally creation,
> When all is subject to annihilation?[15]

Goethe's affirmation of freedom is so powerful in part because it is so honest about its difficulties. And few persons have surpassed Goethe's long-range influence upon our post-modern effort to understand selfhood, perhaps only two—Kierkegaard and, especially, Nietzsche.

Søren Kierkegaard and Friedrich Nietzsche foresaw the weaknesses of Romanticism even as they themselves had felt the difficulties of Rationalism. The most important problems of both alternatives, they thought, was their common assumption that a cosmic structure of meaning, truth, and value is "out there," objectively given either to reason or to feeling. For these prophetic figures, the flights of reason and of feeling are both doomed: the ready-made heaven toward which they soar is not there. We cannot under-stand, as the Greeks had hoped, for we cannot *find* anything to stand under.

Nietzsche's famous phrase, "God is dead," means precisely that the objective structures of meaning and value, whereby Western civilization has guided itself until now, have vanished. We cannot prove them with reason. We cannot hold them with feeling. Seeing this, Nietzsche can already write a history of what is yet to happen, namely, the "advent of Nihilism."[16] Nihilism is the disappearance of externally-given values. The post-modern age has begun. Nietzsche's "Parable of the Madman" is an exposition of the horrifying and bewildering rootlessness of life lived in this absence:

What did we do when we unchained this earth from its sun? Whither is it moving now? Whither are we moving now? Away from all suns? Are we not perpetually falling? Backward, sideward, forward, in all directions? Is there any up or down left? Are we not straying as through an infinite nothing? Do we not feel the breath of empty space?[17]

Nothing can be more terrible than the experience of nihilism, Nietzsche says. But he also says that nothing can be greater, for, because of our nihilism, "Whoever will be born after us . . . will be part of a higher history than all history hitherto."[18] It is apparent that Nietzsche seeks to prepare the way for some sort of cultural and spiritual reconstruction. He insists that "we must first experience Nihilism," yet he also tells us that "sooner or later we shall be in need of new values."[19]

How shall we obtain these "new values"? Finding both classical alternatives to be untenable (though not, on that account, wholly useless), Nietzsche and Kierkegaard exemplify a version of the Hebraic option. It is a drastic revision of this option, of course, for in our post-modern situation "God has died," as Nietzsche would say. Hence no longer can human choosing confidently occur under the self-evident direction of divine law. Even if there is a divine will, as Kierkegaard affirmed, it is not self-evident and the choices made before it are hardly serene. "My doubt is terrible," the Christian theist Kierkegaard writes. "Nothing can withstand it—it is a cursed hunger and I can swallow up every argument, every consolation and sedative—I rush at 10,000 miles a second through every obstacle."[20]

In Nietzsche and Kierkegaard we find the Hebrew view of the self without the corresponding Hebrew confidence in an objectively-given, personally-ordered cosmic law. If God had been the ground of our affirmation of meaning and value, and if now "God is dead," then there seems to be but one way remaining to "give the earth its meaning."[21] As Nietzsche brazenly puts it, "we must become gods." By this he indicates that the creative ground of meaning and value is now to be located in the human will, in human freedom. We must see that in Nietzsche's sense, Kierkegaard, too, dares to "become a god." Kierkegaard wills that there be a God; indeed, he wills that there *really* be a God. But that does not make Kierkegaard's decision, and all that follows from it, any less daring and groundless than Nietzsche's. For both, what we affirm to be meaningful is rooted finally in our own creative willing.

Three ways of self-understanding, with their respective "self" and "world" components, were inherited from the ancient world. Of these, it would appear, only the "self" component of the Hebraic alternative remains for the twentieth century. Reason and feeling have failed to provide the central focus of selfhood, and the objective certitudes they had presupposed seem to have vanished. Apparently, only the human will remains as a possible point of departure. Now, mirroring the creative freedom of the Hebrew God, Adam must "name the animals." Or Adam must try.

Few *answers* to our questions about freedom are given to us by these voices from the nineteenth century. One senses that they, especially Nietzsche, were not entirely sure that there are answers—answers, say, to questions about the relationship of creative freedom to cultural conditioning and to transcendent norms, about the extent of freedom, and even about the precise nature of freedom. They were only sure that, for the sake of our future, freedom must be explored. In view of the history we have traced, this, their single certitude, seems to be a reasonable one.

We cannot avoid the perplexities of freedom left to us from the nineteenth century by retreating to an earlier age.[22] And we cannot move beyond these perplexities except by beginning with them. Hence the task of understanding freedom and appraising its worth does seem to have fallen to us uniquely. It is our peculiar vocation. That does not mean that our task is somehow eccentric, an irregular and presumably erroneous kink in the historical process, as some assert.[23] Perhaps it is, but the contrary case is a strong one, as we have seen in this chapter. There is no reason to belittle our task. But neither is there reason to claim too much for it. We need not claim that if we fail history will end. We need not pretend to know that reason and feeling will never again gain primacy in a viable self-understanding. We need not claim that the posing of the question of freedom in our time is the grand goal of world history until now. We need only to acknowledge that, whatever its cosmic proportions, the question of freedom presents itself to us with singular urgency and that we shall accept its challenge, believing that in our time the pursuit of its answer may tell us who we are.

Notes

1. The heuristic purpose of the scheme developed in this chapter may be clarified by quoting the following words of Robert N. Bellah:

> Of course the scheme itself is not intended as an adequate description of historical reality. Particular lines of ... development cannot simply be forced into the terms of the scheme.... So what I shall present is not intended as a procrustean bed into which the facts of history are to be forced but a theoretical construction against which the historical facts may be illuminated (*Beyond Belief: Essays on Religion in a Post-Traditional World* [New York: Harper & Row, 1970], pp. 24f.)

2. See Karl Jaspers, *The Origin and Goal of History* (New Haven: Yale University Press, 1953), pp. 1–21.

3. Hanna Arendt, *The Human Condition* (Chicago: University of Chicago Press, 1958), p. 15.

4. Rudolf Bultmann makes this same point: ". . . for the ancient Greek world, because the divinity of the *cosmos* and the order prevailing in it was an accepted fact reason [or "true freedom," which is Bultmann's underlying topic] meant a contemplative perception and not a creative constructive process." (*Essays: Philosophical and Theological* [New York: Macmillan, 1955], p. 322.)

5. Herbert J. Muller, *Freedom in the Ancient World* (New York: Harper, 1961), pp. 168, 202.

6. Cf. Bultmann, *Essays: Philosophical and Theological,* p. 308.

7. This statement is Paulo Freire's (in *Pedagogy of the Oppressed* [New York: Seabury, 1974], p. 76; italics removed), though he is not intending by it to be describing the Hebraic conception.

8. Richard L. Rubenstein, *After Auschwitz* (Indianapolis: Bobbs-Merrill, 1966), esp. ch. 5 and 6.

9. Augustine, "On Free Will," in *Earlier Writings,* ed. J. H. Burleigh, Library of Christian Classics, Vol. 6 (Philadelphia: Westminster Press, 1963), pp. 204, 210, 213.

10. Quoted in James Bruce Ross and Mary Martin McLaughlin, eds., *The Portable Renaissance Reader* (New York: Viking, 1953), p. 478; italics added.

11. G. W. F. Hegel, *Lectures on the Philosophy of Religion* (London: Routledge & Kegan Paul, 1962), p. 275.

12. Walter Kaufmann, trans., *Goethe's Faust* (Garden City, N.Y.: Anchor Books, 1963), p. 187.

13. Ibid., p. 467.

14. Ibid., p. 469.

15. Ibid., p. 471.

16. Friedrich Nietzsche, *The Will to Power* (London: Allen and Unwin, 1924), Vol. 1, p. 1; quoted in Walter Kaufmann, ed., *Existentialism from Dostoevsky to Sartre,* rev. ed. (New York: New American Library, 1975), p. 130.

17. Friedrich Nietzsche, *The Joyful Science* (London: Allen and Unwin, 1914), pp. 167–69; reprinted in Walter Kaufmann, ed., *Existentialism,* pp. 126f.

18. Nietzsche, *The Joyful Science,* p. 168; reprinted in Walter Kaufmann, ed., *Existentialism,* p. 126.

19. Nietzsche, *Will to Power,* p. 2.

20. Quoted in Robert Bretall, ed., *A Kierkegaard Anthology* (New York: Modern Library, 1938), p. 14.

21. Friedrich Nietzsche, *Thus Spoke Zarathustra,* trans. R. J. Hollingdale (Baltimore: Penguin Books, 1961), p. 102.

22. This point is made by Bultmann, in *Essays: Philosophical and Theological,* pp. 312–14.

23. Cf. James F. Ross, a Review Article on *God and the World* by John B. Cobb, Jr. (Philadelphia: Westminster, 1969), *Journal of the American Academy of Religion* 38 (September 1970): 313.

Chapter Two

The Nature of Freedom: A Philosophical Perspective

If we are to assess freedom from the standpoint of faith, we must be clear about what it is we are assessing. In order to arrive at an adequate view of freedom we will begin with that conception developed in the early work of the French existentialist philosopher, Jean-Paul Sartre. We will then examine the way Sartre came to modify his early view, his reason for this modification, and its logical outcome.

There are several advantages in following this course of discussion. First, it provides historical continuity in as much as Sartre's work stands directly and consciously in the tradition of Nietzsche, whose moral vision we met in the previous chapter. No one has more clearly worked to accomplish what Nietzsche claimed was needed if Western civilization is to survive. Secondly, proceeding in this way allows us to start with a reasonably common concept of freedom. Sartre's views on the meaning of freedom probably have wider currency today than those of any alternative. The fact that Sartre's philosophy is not as much talked about as it once was only means, I think, that his views have in many respects become the new orthodoxy, even when those views are but vaguely understood. Thirdly, Sartre's is clearly a "secular" notion of freedom in almost any sense of that term. Beginning with such a view, devoid as it is of theistic or religious sympathies, enables us to confront the problem of relating faith and freedom in its most extreme form. Finally, and most important, Sartre's own self-correcting analysis is enormously instructive, leading us much of the way toward a more fully adequate understanding of freedom than that with which Sartre began. Later in this chapter I shall claim that the framework of A. N. Whitehead's philosophy allows for a better articulation of this fuller view of freedom, one which combines the crucial elements of Sartre's early "existentialism" as well as his later version of "Marxism." But I do not begin with Whitehead's philosophy precisely because to do so would be to sacrifice the advantages I have just mentioned.

The final section of this chapter discusses the elements of a satisfactory view of freedom, as these have been gleaned from an examination of Sartre and Whitehead. The reader who is not attuned to the complexities of philosophical discussion (though I have tried to keep them at a minimum) may wish to turn immediately to this concluding section.

21

Sartre's Existentialism

Western thought generally has understood the most basic human reality, frequently called the "ego" or the "I," to be something which endures throughout one's individual history. A person has successive experiences, possesses various qualities, and performs actions, but the person's fundamental reality somehow stands under and owns these experiences, qualities, and actions. The essential self is the abiding ego which traverses the variations of one's historic existence.

Sartre shares with others certain objections to this notion of the self. One objection is the fact that we have no introspective evidence of an enduring, essential ego. Our primitive self-awareness reveals a succession of experiences, feelings, and actions, but it does not reveal an underlying "I" which has the experiences and does the actions.[1] Another objection is the scientific uselessness of an abiding essence, either for individuals or for humanity as such. We need not ignore certain structural commonalities, some of which may persist universally for long periods of time, in order to acknowledge the basic plasticity of human beings as revealed in anthropological and psychological studies.[2] A third objection is more obscure, perhaps, but also more central to Sartre's position. If the most basic self is fixed and abiding, how can we speak of the freedom and self-creativity of that self? Sartre, in particular, thinks that the intrusion of a fixed essence into selfhood would "congeal" the self, eliminating its spontaneity.[3] Our actions would follow in computer-like fashion from our fixed nature in its intercourse with the world given to it. How can we explain the self-generativity of the self—its spontaneity and creative initiative—if the self is a fixed and finished substance? The idea of something established and enduring describes a stone better than it describes the fundamental self with which we are familiar.

The elements of Sartre's alternative conception of selfhood appeared early in his book *The Transcendence of the Ego.* The fundamental givens of human reality are twofold, the objects for consciousness, and consciousness itself. Consciousness, however, is not a thing; indeed, "in a sense, it is a nothing."[4] It is no-thing in the sense of not having or even being an identifiable essence or fixed nature. Unlike the concrete world given to it, consciousness is freedom conceived in its most radical form—it is spontaneous, indeterminate, ceaseless creativity. Sartre writes:

> Consciousness is an impersonal spontaneity. It determines its existence at each instant, without our being able to conceive of anything *before* it. Thus each instant of our conscious life reveals to us a creation *ex nihilo.* Not a new *arrangement,* but a new existence.[5]

What we ordinarily call the "ego" or "I" is not directly given in human reality, according to Sartre. The ego is evident only indirectly, through an act of consciousness; in fact, the ego is an object for consciousness that is constituted *by* consciousness.[6] Immediately, we are prone to wonder why consciousness creates for itself an ego, a mask of "essencehood." Sartre's reply is that "consciousness is frightened by its own spontaneity. . . ."[7] "There is something distressing for each of us, to catch in the act this tireless creation of which *we* are not the creators."[8] Spontaneity opens up a "vertigo of possibility" beyond one's own confident control. Seeing itself as perpetually unsettled, desirous of escaping from threatening indeterminateness into the security of fixed stability, consciousness creates the "mask" of an ego, "as if to make the ego its guardian and its law," behind which it may hide itself—from itself![9]

Because consciousness creates the ego, or the "I," and not vice versa, Sartre must deny that consciousness is personal, that I can say it is *my* consciousness. He also wants to deny, however, that consciousness is consciousness-in-general. Unable to appeal to some underlying ego as the principle of individuation, Sartre locates the unity of consciousness in the synthetic character of consciousness itself. "Consciousness . . . can be limited only by itself. Thus, it constitutes a synthetic and individual totality entirely isolated from other totalities of the same type."[10] In this sense consciousness creates its own distinct identity. But consciousness is not entirely isolated; Sartre also says that consciousness "unifies itself, concretely, by a play of 'transversal' intentionalities which are concrete and real *retentions of past consciousness.*"[11] This recognition that consciousness is social—now, however, only with respect to other, past consciousnesses—is an important qualification.

The social character of consciousness is also manifest in a presupposition which Sartre takes from Edmund Husserl, the father of phenomenology, the presupposition that "all consciousness is consciousness *of* something."[12] Consciousness without an object is inconceivable; it is always "being-in-the-world."[13] However, the "nothingness" of consciousness always, in a sense, "surpass(es) the real," as Sartre says in a later work.[14] This surpassing strengthens the social character of consciousness, for, in surpassing the real, consciousness makes of it a world. There is, to be sure, a sheer givenness, a "facticity" as Sartre calls it, which is not dependent upon consciousness. But it is consciousness, as imagination, that constitutes the given to be a *world*. In Sartre's analysis, then, "world" and "consciousness" are interdependent realities; in this sense they are "social."

Being and Nothingness[15] is the culmination of Sartre's early thinking. Any differences it reflects are but nuances which result from the fact that Sartre now contrasts consciousness and the given in the starkest possible terms. It is the total emptiness of the given, now termed "being-in-itself," that becomes more prominent. Conceived of in itself, were that possible, being-in-itself is entirely devoid of meaning and value. Consciousness, termed "being-for-itself," is ceaseless creativity, it is pure freedom. In each moment consciousness is an unfinishedness seeking achievement. Sartre calls this pursuit a "project." The project is to be understood primarily in terms of giving significance—meaning and value—to the world. But precisely because consciousness is the source of all norms, it, as meaning-giving activity, cannot be justified by any norms or values beyond itself. Thus Sartre gives rigorous philosophical expression to Nietzsche's insistence that "only through evaluation is there value: and without evaluation the nut of existence would be hollow."[16] And because our creative freedom is the only source of earthly significance, Sartre also echoes Nietzsche's plea:

> Stay loyal to the earth, my brothers. . . . Do not let (your virtue) . . . fly away from the things of earth and beat with its wings against the eternal walls. . . . Lead, as I do, the flown-away virtue back to earth—yes, back to body and life: that it may give the earth its meaning, a human meaning.[17]

The enormous sensitivity with which Sartre derives his categories from introspective analysis, and the searing power with which he uses this scheme to illuminate personal and interpersonal human existence, has made *Being and Nothingness* a monument of profundity. No other philosopher has so adroitly combined complex ontological analysis with moving revelations of the meaning of being human. In particular, no one else has given so bold a picture of human freedom as creativity, the source of all meaning and value.

Sartre's Marxism

The power of Sartre's early analysis did not hide its problematic features, even, as it turned out, from Sartre himself. The most important difficulty for our purposes is the problem of the relatedness of consciousness or the self. We have been at pains to point out the social character of the self for the early Sartre. This characteristic is frequently ignored by readers of Sartre, largely no doubt because his own terminology tended to obscure it. Sartre said consciousness is influenced by its own past,[18] for example, but this was consigned to oblivion by his stronger and more persistent claim that each movement of consciousness is a creation *ex nihilo*.[19] Moreover, the relatedness of the self to its world, though clear, was purely formal. Consciousness must have some world as its intended object, but the nature of that world seemed in no way to influence how it was intended, beyond defining the possible alternatives for the self's constitutive activity. In fact, however, the past actual world appears to do more than that; it seems to us also to have an influence on which of those possibilities are actualized in the present. The political possibilities abstractly present in a repressive society are not equally "real." The givenness of a racist society may allow a multitude of possibilities for self-understanding, theoretically, but that givenness does more than merely specify what things are possible; it somehow seems to weight the constitutive activity of consciousness toward certain options and away from others. For such reasons, the freedom of consciousness in the early Sartre seemed too pure to many of his readers, too unrelated to the formative power of its social and natural context.

More recently Sartre has recognized that this criticism is correct. His later work, in fact, may be viewed in part as his effort to deal with what we have called the problem of the social relatedness of consciousness or freedom. Programmatically, this effort, appearing in *Search for a Method,* occurs as an attempt to relate his early existentialism to Marxism. Indeed, so intent is he to open his previous conclusions to the concrete dimensions of our corporate existence, which he sees to be the object of Marxist analysis, that Sartre is now prepared to place existentialism as a fragment within the more comprehensive system of Marxism. Existentialism, he says, is to be discarded when it has led Marxist reflection to return to the humanistic awareness from which it came.[20]

Sartre's version of Marxism is summarized in a dictum he recalls from Engels: "It is men themselves who make their history, but within a given environment which conditions them. . . ."[21] True Marxism, Sartre insists, always recognizes in human action a margin of concreteness—the "profundity of the lived" he calls it in one place[22]—not reducible to nature and culture.[23] The orthodox or "lazy" Marxism of contemporary thinkers has either neglected this surplusage altogether or assigned it to chance.[24] Thus neglecting the uniqueness of human agency, the concrete reality of purposes or aims (i.e., "final causes") has also been overlooked.[25] If these errors are corrected, materialism will not be reductionistic;[26] instead it will be the generalization, formulated by Marx himself, that "the mode of production of material life generally dominates the development of social, political, and intellectual life."[27]

Although "material life" does not wholly determine human belief and action, in order to allow that it even "dominates" these dimensions of our existence Sartre must introduce important changes into his earlier existentialism. He does, but the basic understanding of human reality remains much the same. There is no human essence, only structural commonalities making possible an " 'ideology' of existence."[28] We create ourselves by our projects.[29] The project, however, is no longer viewed as freedom's creation *ex nihilo;* instead, the structure of the project—or praxis, as Sartre now calls it—is held to be "need."[30] Need is both a lack *and* an impulse to go beyond that lack.[31] It is therefore a given for praxis and an impetus to praxis. Need does not determine or explain one's self-making. Need "conditions" praxis, it urges or lures.[32] Thus need renders the range of possibility confronting a person to be, not "a zone of indetermination, but rather a strongly structured region which depends upon all of History and which includes its own contradictions."[33] Translated into socio-economic categories, need becomes "scarcity," and the point of contact with Marxism is clear. It is, nevertheless, a humanistic Marxism, refusing to be reductionistic. For example:

> Exploiter and exploited are men in conflict in a system whose principal characteristic is *scarcity*. To be sure, the capitalist owns the instruments of labor, and the worker does not own them: there we have a pure contradiction. But to be precise, this contradiction *never succeeds in accounting for each event*. It is the *framework* for the event. . . .[34]

Sartre's combination of existentialism and Marxism enables each to enrich the other. From Marxism comes a contextual consciousness, an awareness that the self's freedom cannot be divorced from its framework of material or concrete possibilities. The range of possibilities, derived from one's past, emerges as an ordered structure of opportunities for future becoming. The future is not an addition to the present; it is already ingredient in the present as its goal.[35] We define ourselves by our projects; nevertheless, our projects can only be chiseled out of the rock of real, and not merely abstract, possibilities for future actualization. Therefore, Sartre can also say that the "future defines the individual."[36] A Marxist existentialism sees how the past enriches or impoverishes our future, and, consequently, how the future extends or restricts the quality of our freedom in the present.

From existentialism Sartre's synthesis gains an awareness of the irreducible efficacy of human purpose. The "bad faith" of orthodox Marxists has been the vacillation of their historical explanations between efficient causes and final causes in order to suit their a priori myths.[37] To explain human actions fully in terms of efficient causality is neither Marxist nor scientific.

> It was legitimate for the natural sciences to free themselves from the anthropomorphism which consists in bestowing human properties on inanimate objects. But it is perfectly absurd to assume by analogy the same scorn for anthropomorphism where anthropology is concerned. When one is studying man, what can be more exact or more rigorous than to *recognize human properties in him*? The simple inspection of the social field ought to have led to the discovery that the relation to ends is a permanent structure of human enterprises and that it is *on the basis of this relation* that real men evaluate actions, institutions, or economic constructions. It ought to have been established that our comprehension of the other is necessarily attained through ends.[38]

Sartre has thus become committed to the construction of a philosophy of human freedom that recognizes both external conditioning and the individual's creative self-making. The key to his effort is the notion of need, as we have seen. Freedom is experienced cast in the inclining aura of need. In this way, Sartre ties freedom to its environment, for, as Hazel

Barnes has said, need "brings in something from the outside . . . which man cannot ultimately escape, no matter how much he may vary his reaction to it."[39]

If Sartre's concept of need solves the problem of social relatedness noted earlier, it would seem, however, to be an incomplete solution. How is it, we must ask, that the social and material context creates needs? How is it that needs are not only "lacks" (the absence of realization) but also aspirations (the impetus toward actualization)? Why are needs cast in an aura of inclination?

This kind of question is important for any program that seeks to ground human freedom securely in a material context. The task is to understand freedom as being essentially affected by external circumstance—diversity or conformity, poverty or plenty, liberty or slavery. Otherwise, one would have one's freedom regardless of external conditions; the connection between freedom and, say, economic security would merely be a "habit of the mind." Sartre's move to Marxism is a rejection of so ephemeral a freedom. Social and economic conditions create needs, not merely because we happen to think that they do, but because such conditions somehow exercise real agency even over freedom. Our question is, how?

Sartre cannot answer this question; he works with a view of nature that admits of no solution. He continues to understand the physical world as being composed of detached, self-contained, and passive bits of matter. Nature is part of what Sartre calls "being-in-itself," the brute givenness of things devoid of meaning and value. How can a valueless given be of value to freedom, positively or negatively, unless freedom arbitrarily constitutes it as such? How can a given that is passive *create* needs?

For Sartre, in sum, the world given to consciousness stands powerless before consciousness, making no demands and claiming no obligations. Why then does freedom not constitute material oppression to be enriching and impoverishment to be fulfilling? With Sartre's view of nature, need can only be grounded in the constitutive power of consciousness, not in the material conditions of nature and society. In the final analysis, need is entirely a creation of subjectivity. And the decision of oppressed subjectivity can be no more instructive, no more legitimate, than that of its oppressor.

Interestingly, Marx's own view of nature was more adequate than is that of most of his followers, including Sartre. In the *Theses on Feuerbach*, Marx complains that "all previous materialism . . . (conceives of) things, reality, the sensible world . . . only in the form of *objects*, or of observation, but not as *sensuous* human activity, praxis " (First Thesis). Marx himself is here reflecting a more classical view of matter. The Aristotelian tradition had viewed matter as potentiality, thus ensuring a place for activity in its conception of nature; a natural thing, in part material, is by its very nature in process, possessing within itself a principle of agency. In the sixteenth and seventeenth centuries, however, there emerged a new view which identified the physical world with matter, and, more significantly, deemed matter to be wholly actual and thus in itself changeless.[40] For the new view, matter is movable but contains within itself no principle of motion. Consciousness, as self-creative and dynamic subjectivity, must be wholly removed from the inert physical world. Thus there arose the Cartesian dualism of mind and matter with its concomitant problems. These problems recur in Sartre's Cartesianism. How can a passive physical environment impose needs upon the free, self-creative self, as Sartre now wishes to say? They cannot. Judgments of value, including those pertaining to need, are impositions of an active subjectivity upon a passive material world. And, as we have seen, on this view the judgments of the oppressed are no less arbitrary than those of the oppressor.

A Whiteheadian Synthesis

Roger Garaudy has observed that Marxist thought since Lenin has generally failed to incorporate into itself the advances of the sciences.[41] This is unfortunate; the more recent conceptions of nature, if heeded, might have prevented Marxism from degenerating into the reductionistic determinism that has characterized so much of its history. But of more significance for our consideration, these conceptions of the material world provide a basis for Sartre's doctrine of need. That this is true is nowhere better illustrated than in the work of Alfred N. Whitehead.

The seventeenth-century view, Whitehead observes, held that nature is "composed of permanent things, namely bits of matter, moving about in space which is otherwise empty."[42] The crucial assumption here is the "independent individuality of each bit of matter. Each stone is conceived as fully describable apart from any reference to any other portion of matter. It might be alone in the Universe, . . . but it would still be the stone which it is, . . . adequately described without any reference to past or future."[43]

Whitehead, like others, has argued extensively for the scientific inadequacy, not to say incoherence, of this point of view.[44] He also sees it to be a powerful opponent of the "presuppositions of humanism."[45] Valuation, purposing, and subjectivity—all essential to our sense of selfhood—are rendered alien, needless intrusions of dubious reality. If retained at all, they are housed in a dualism which makes judgments of meaning and value either irrelevant to the material environment or arbitrary impositions upon it. The impasse arising in Sartre's attempted move to Marxism is an illustration of Whitehead's point. Dead, relationless matter knows no needs, conveys no aspirations.

The more recent conception of nature, Whitehead says,

> . . . is expressed in terms of energy, activity, and the whole vibratory differentiations of space-time. Any local agitation shakes the whole universe. The

distant effects are minute, but they are there. The . . . group of agitations which we term matter is fused into its environment. There is no possibility of a detached, self-contained local existence. The environment enters into the nature of each thing. Some elements in the nature of a complete set of agitations may remain stable as those agitations are propelled through a changing environment. But such a stability is only the case in a general, average way. This average fact is the reason why we find the same chair, the same rock and the same planet, enduring for days, or for centuries, or for millions of years. In this average fact the time-factor takes the aspect of endurance, and change is a detail. The fundamental fact, according to the physics of the present day, is that the environment with its peculiarities seeps into the group-agitation which we term matter, and the group-agitations extend their character to the environment.[46]

On this view, nature is vibrantly alive. Natural objects are composed of minute, momentary quanta of energetic activity. Each energetic occasion is dynamic, a creative synthesis that is something more than the sum of the elements synthesized. In addition, each such unit is relational; it is finally incomprehensible apart from the past occasions which contribute to its contents and influence its aim, and from the future onto which it projects itself. Therefore, each quantum makes a difference, however infinitesimal, to the character of the cosmic process. It accepts and adapts the past, and imposes its adaptation of inherited data upon subsequent occasions, which in turn receive, synthesize, and project. In this sense, one may say that each unit of energetic activity is an evaluation. Nietzsche's claim, so central to Sartre's thinking, is apropos, too, of Whitehead's view: "Only through evaluation is there value." Values are not simply human impositions. Nature, too, is evaluative. Valuations are givens.

Needs, being the appetitive entertainment of unrealized possibility, are a form of valuation. Thus, needs, too, are given in the nature of things. Like other data inherited from the past, they are, as Sartre says, a part of "the framework for the event" in the present; that is, they influence, but do not determine, the presently becoming synthesis. Past valuations of needfulness are, as it were, allegations of oughtness weighing heavily upon the present, which now must be ratified or revised. Needs are not arbitrary creations of human freedom in an otherwise needless world. The natural and social context of each event of creative self-making is alive with needful propensities.

We have seen that the view of nature Whitehead describes and defends makes possible Sartre's effort to incorporate a Marxist dimension into his thought. It shows how creative freedom is inextricably dependent on and embedded in its material environment. It does so, however, without compromising Sartre's emphasis upon the freedom and creativity of the self. We must now underscore this point.

Whitehead focuses upon the continuities between the quanta of energy constituting the physical world and the discrete moments of human experience in the life of the mind. Each type of event is an "actual entity," Whitehead's term for the basic spatio-temporal atoms constituting reality. Actual entities differ almost infinitely in degree, though not in kind. In various combinations, called "societies," they compose the objects we encounter in our ordinary experience.

Whitehead shows, first, that the actual entities constituting reality at every level are relational or social. This means, for one thing, that the ingredients—the "what"—of each presently becoming actual entity is dependent upon the actualities and latent possibilities given in the past, immediate and remote. The relational character of actual entities also means that the way these ingredients are synthesized in the present—the "how"—is contributed to by the past. But there is novelty as well as repetition in the temporal process. Whitehead believes that novelty, on the physical level as well as in "mental" processes, is best accounted for by attributing to all actual entities at least some miniscule measure of self-directedness.

In addition to being relational, therefore, Whitehead also argues that actual entities are autonomous. They are not socially related and autonomous in precisely the same respects, of course, and the balance of sociality and autonomy varies enormously among actual entities. Repetition, and thus social dependence, dominates overwhelmingly in the actual entities making up physical processes or what we ordinarily call "nature." Here the capacity for novelty, and thus the exercise of autonomy, remains for the most part unactualized potentiality. In "higher" or more complex processes, and especially in the self, the measure of autonomy becomes an increasingly significant factor, interfaced with the inheritance of the past upon the present becoming. Here, particularly, the power of the past upon the present is that of influence—the "power of persuasion," Whitehead sometimes calls it—and not determination.

Here more than one consequence remains genuinely possible. We know this to be the case in our immediate self-awareness, or so we believe until the enormous success of deterministic models in the physical sciences causes us to think otherwise. However, in the physical sciences (physics, especially) the deterministic model has now given way to a looser, more dynamic conception of physical relationships. This development strengthens the notion that freedom and creativity—in some very embryonic form, no doubt—characterizes the entire physical process, physical as well as mental. This notion is further strengthened if we assume, as apparently we must, that the mind is part of nature. For if this is true, the autonomy so central to our intuitive understanding of mentality tells us something about the nature of things no less than does the repetition that dominates physical processes. Both sociality, with its predominance of repetition, and autonomy, with its attendant character of novelty, are ingredient throughout the natural order. There is no question, then, about creative freedom at the level of the autonomous self.

This discussion of Whitehead's viewpoint has been selective as well as nontechnical. For a consideration of larger issues related to Whitehead's philosophy the reader must turn elsewhere.[47] Our purpose here has been to show that Whitehead's philosophy can give to Sartre's understanding of freedom the cosmological setting that it requires in order to gain coherence. We turn now to a discussion of the elements of freedom suggested by this understanding and, if it is adequate, by our common human experience.

Elements of Freedom

In the preceding sections we have followed the development of Sartre's idea of freedom. Sartre had begun by understanding freedom to be autonomous self-creation. In this respect he gave expression to a view central to that tradition of Western thought stemming from Hebrew experience and coming to special focus in Nietzsche. Under the influence of Marxism, however, Sartre came to see that it is not possible to think of freedom in total isolation from some material or social context. He then began to emphasize the material framework that "conditions" but does not determine creative freedom. This raised two questions. How can the material world, which on Sartre's view is inert and passive, be said to condition or act upon freedom? Moreover, how can the self be conditioned without its freedom being eliminated? Answers to both questions, we suggested, become available to us in the conceptuality provided by Whitehead. Thus we concluded that it is possible to speak both of freedom's autonomous creativity and of freedom's conditioning context. Freedom, then, has two polar elements, creativity and context. We shall speak first of the former.

What is creativity? All talk of creativity must remain at the level of suggestive imagery. We cannot characterize creativity by reducing it to those ingredients constituting it because creativity, as such, constitutes itself. Nor can we understand creativity by looking to its antecedent determinates because, finally, creativity determines itself. Creativity in itself cannot be defined, it can only be suggested.[48] Even so, the task is not a hopeless one, if Sartre is right, for the simple reason that what is being suggested in our verbal imagery is a mode of reality which, in some sense, we as subjects of experience already are. Thus, speech about creativity will seek to direct our attention to that with which we are in some way already familiar.

Creativity, we are frequently told, is spontaneity; it is a striving, a pursuit of newness. It is the past bursting its bounds. It is making something out of nothing. Creativity is that plunging into the future which breaks open the barriers of the given and dares to make real that which is only dimly hoped for. It is making something new.[49]

Such language leads us, first, to moments in our experience when spontaneity seems to prevail, as in a sudden uninhibited expression of delight or in the impulsive joy of a child vicariously shared. Chance seems to pervade such moments. It is necessary to add, however, that the apparent creature of chance "fits," it has such a propriety that the experience seems "at home" with us and we with it. This aspect of familiarity may be what makes it appropriate to talk, secondly, of striving when we consider creativity. Hence the notion of spontaneity is combined with intentionality, purposing, resolve.[50] We are thus led to search for moments in experience where there is a peculiar joining of the two, where resolve begets spontaneity and, in turn, spontaneity strengthens purpose so that the two flow together, enhancing one another.

Finally, discussions of creativity usually make mention of newness. But we must be careful here. Newness refers to that which is not yet. More basically, however, it means that which is not simply an extrapolation from the past, that which comes into being finally (though not solely) as a result of human agency. It is important to realize that this tells us nothing in particular about the pattern of that which is new, i.e., whether it is novel or repetitious. It may not resemble or preserve the old, but then again it may.[51] The point is that creativity is not antithetical to conserving the past, just as it is not subject to the dictates of the past. This is the case because newness pertains primarily to aesthetic ownership. It is "my" achievement of feeling—*this* is what has not been until now. "Original" or not, I act to own it, accept responsibility for it, identify myself with it. Only secondarily might it be the case that an achievement that is thus made "me" or "mine" is also an achievement that displays novelty of content or originality. Unless we understand this, creativity is likely to be viewed either as the possession of an elite few, or as the masses' frenzied pursuit of novel content for its own sake. In either instance creativity is reduced to mere change, and the *self*-agency of the creative event is ignored; there remains only the search for novelty, a search ironically dominated by external circumstance. Fundamentally, creativity must be viewed as an essential element of *every* human event, however much (and for whatever reason) it might have been repressed and obscured.[52]

Creativity is not a luxury that the practical pursuit of freedom can dispense with. Too frequently freedom is considered solely in negative terms, as the absence of unwanted or impoverishing restraint. The contextual nature of freedom necessarily gives to considerations of this negative side of freedom a strategic primacy. Nevertheless, the incompleteness of a negative understanding of freedom is manifest again and again in social history: the binding conditions have been removed, but the emptiness remains. Why? Because freedom is something more than an unfettering from bondage. Thus the pursuit of human liberation requires something more as well. It requires more than the elimination of repres-

sion. It requires more than an environment rich with alternative poten-
tials. It requires more than the realization of a stage in evolution where
creativity is merely possible. It requires, in addition, the actual emergence
of creativity, for which each of the preceding conditions is necessary but
not sufficient. Is it possible to teach, to cultivate creativity beyond the
provision of these conditions? Perhaps; certainly Paulo Freire's "pedagogy of the oppressed" gives some hope that in principle at least, this is
possible.[53] In any case, how to nurture creativity is a question integral to
the comprehensive pursuit of a liberated existence, and it is a question to
which Christianity claims to speak, as we shall see.

Context is the other polar element of freedom. If, as we have been
saying, a liberated environment rich in possibility is not a sufficient condition of creativity and hence of freedom, such a context remains an absolutely necessary prerequisite of liberated life. Ideologies of the privileged
classes carefully ignore this fact, pretending instead that the quality of
freedom is a constant, unaffected by external circumstance. The power of
Marxism lies in its uncontrovertible denial of this fiction and in its profound (though not infallible) analysis of the ways in which context affects
creativity. Ideologies of the privileged presuppose a Cartesian dualism
and its supposition that the creative mind is wholly explicable without
reference to its material environment. This assumption can even be made
to sound humane, for when it is coupled with the supposition that the
impact of context upon creativity is either "all" or "none," it then is
presented as the only means of denying that the power of the environment over the mind is complete. The tendency of what Sartre calls "lazy"
Marxism toward determinism has reinforced the prevalence of this
dichotomy in the modern discussion. Sartre's version of Marxism, integrated into a Whiteheadian understanding of nature, avoids this dichotomy. It enables us to see that, as Sartre says, the context is a
"framework" that "conditions" but does not determine creativity.

The context is the immediate and distant past, the circumstances that
"stand around" the present decision, coloring it indelibly. The context
includes the purposes and energies of the immediately preceding moment of experience, summing up the more remote past, and then pushing
the structure of valuations there developed into the present. The conditioning context includes our bodies with their own more or less automatic
capabilities as well as their distinctive meanings for us individually. As
Rubem Alves writes:

> Our civilization has tried to convince us that this is not so, that the greater the
> repression of the body, the greater the freedom of the spirit. It is ironical
> that torturers have known more about man than our ideologues. For mil-
> lennia they have known that whoever controls the body has power over the
> personality.[54]

And the conditioning context includes the external world—a physical environment more or less friendly to human survival, a world of economic opportunity and rigid limitation, a social world with its inhibitory stratification, a cultural world with its rich or poor reservoir of felt meanings and envisaged possibilities, and the cross-mingling of these in a complexity that sometimes makes "social" planning little more reliable than sorcery. History makes it clear, Whitehead contends, that a "poverty of life" in these respects weakens almost fatally what he calls the "impulse towards adventure," including that adventure of spirit we have referred to as creativity.[55]

Sometimes the impact of context upon creativity is so massive that, in candor, all talk of human freedom is purely abstract. In such instances we understandably speak of determination or coercion, and much of the ease of life depends on this large margin of habituality in human experience. In the final analysis, however, talk of determination is always relative. Absolute determination, like absolute creativity, is a fiction. Our experience is a reliable guide. We are more than our environment, but we know ourselves to be that, too, in important respects. Our situation in the world with its gifts and restrictions so powerfully insinuates itself into our present becoming that we cannot understand ourselves except as embodied selves, embodied in a physical and cultural circumstance. "The human being is inseparable from its environment in each occasion of its existence."[56]

Creativity and context are the polar elements of freedom. Conceptually, they presuppose each other. They are thus abstractions. In process philosophy there is no context that is not creatively appropriated, however small the margin of creativity. Likewise, there is no creativity that escapes the profound weight of the past, its context, as the source and lure for its present becoming.

It is especially important to recall the abstractness of creativity and context as we turn now to consider the relation of freedom to value.

Sartre, following Nietzsche's lead, locates the origin of value in the evaluative act of the will. To value means to grade, to place a worth on something. A process perspective accepts this analysis and generalizes it (thus balancing its arbitrary subjectivism, as will become apparent). Each basic unit of actuality is relational, appropriating the data for its becoming from the past. Each such unit is also autonomous, determining for itself how that data is to be ordered in the present. Present preferences then become data for future becomings. This rhythmic process—appropriation of context and autonomous self-creation—extends everlastingly. Thus at each point on every level of reality there occurs in some degree an autonomously guided preferential appropriation of the given environment, heightening or diminishing the relevance of inherited data so as to achieve a particular synthesis of the past in the present.

Each basic unit of reality is evaluative. In some measure, therefore, each actuality in the temporal process "gives the earth its meaning," to use Nietzsche's phrase, or, to adopt the language of Genesis, "names the animals." This is preeminently true of human beings. It may be that we do not know of our responsibility in this regard, or that we know but ignore it, or that we actively deceive ourselves about it—to such considerations we shall return later. Regardless, we are, as Sartre so ominously puts it, "condemned" to the role of a creator of values, even if we share that function with God, on the one hand, and entities less complex than ourselves, on the other. One might be tempted to say that the evaluative role of sub-human processes is so minimal by comparison as to be inappropriately coupled with human evaluations. Our recent (re)discovery of the close linkage between our own purposings and those implicit in "lower" forms of life gives the lie to such a narrow purview. The centrality of the human role in the creation of meaning and value is scarcely to be denied; it is, after all, we who contemplate the current ecological crisis. Still, all creation conspires to give the earth some meaning or other; all creatures, in some manner, "name the animals," the human creature especially.

Now, when we consider human freedom simply with respect to its creative dimension it is correct to say, with Sartre, that the evaluations of human freedom are groundless. In this sense nothing justifies or makes right our choices. Evaluations are arbitrary, when so regarded, because any external principle we might appeal to in order to justify our choices has been established as a true criterion by some (logically) prior choice of ours. Sartre's well-known illustration of this is Abraham's choice to sacrifice Isaac. It was Abraham who decided that the angel appearing to him announcing God's will was real and not imagined, and if real, an angel of the Lord and not of Satan, and if of the Lord, a representative of one whose word is worthy to be obeyed. In short, the answer we choose to give to the question of value is grounded in that choice itself. We "name" what is of worth to us. Such is the nature of creativity.

Creativity, however, is not the whole reality of freedom. The polar element in freedom is a material context heavily weighted with the preferences of the past. These inherited evaluations include those of our own immediately preceding moments, those of other human and sub-human actualities, and the pervasive preferences of God. The evaluations derived from the past do not present themselves as mute historical facts, indifferent to their own destiny. Neither, though, do they "determine" present evaluations. They constitute the persuasive framework of such choices. At a level of felt-inheritance, past preferences weigh in upon us demandingly, insistent of their own realization. From the perspective of context, the evaluations of human freedom are far from groundless; quite the contrary, they are givens, built into the nature of things.

We saw earlier that creativity and context, taken by themselves, are abstractions. Each presupposes the other in the full reality of human freedom. The relative efficacy of creativity and context varies markedly in human experience as it does in the full span of the natural order. The balance between our sense of autonomy, deriving from the exercise of creativity, and our sense of being determined, deriving from the power of our material context over us, is by no means a constant one, either. Sometimes the creative pole, and thus the awareness of autonomy, dominates. Sometimes context overwhelms us, and thus the feeling of being formed by our past. Often the blend of the two baffles self-analysis. "I choose," we may wish to say of such times, "yet not I but the past that lives within me."

Notes

1. Jean-Paul Sartre, *The Transcendence of the Ego* (New York: Noonday, 1957), pp. 47ff. Much of the material in this and the next two sections appeared previously in my "Sartre on the Self and Society: A Whiteheadian View of Sartre's Later Philosophy," *Southwestern Journal of Philosophy* 7 (Fall 1976): 65–76.

2. Jean-Paul Sartre, *Search for a Method* (New York: Vintage, 1968), pp. 169f.

3. *Transcendence of the Ego,* pp. 41f.

4. Ibid., p. 93.

5. Ibid., p. 98f.

6. Ibid., pp. 53, 60–93.

7. Ibid., p. 100.

8. Ibid., p. 99.

9. See ibid., pp. 100–102.

10. Ibid., p. 39.

11. Ibid.; italics added.

12. Ibid., p. 44.

13. Jean-Paul Sartre, *Psychology of the Imagination* (New York: Philosophical Library, 1946), pp. 208f.

14. Ibid., p. 208; italics removed. For the details of Sartre's analysis, see pp. 11–24 and 201–211.

15. Jean-Paul Sartre, *Being and Nothingness* (Secaucus, N.J.: Citadel Press, 1965).

16. Friedrich Nietzsche, *Thus Spoke Zarathustra* (Baltimore: Penguin Books, 1961), p. 85.

17. Ibid., p. 102. Cf. *The Flies* for Sartre's dramatic elaboration of this theme, in Jean-Paul Sartre, *No Exit and Three Other Plays* (New York: Vintage Books, 1955), pp. 50–127.

18. Sartre, *Transcendence of the Ego,* p. 39.

19. Ibid., pp. 98f.

20. Sartre, *Search for a Method,* pp. 8, 18.

21. Quoted in ibid., p. 31; cf. p. xviii.

22. Ibid., p. 145.

23. See, e.g., ibid., pp. 26f., 29.

24. Cf. ibid., pp. 27f., 29, 37ff., 53, 82, 115, 124.

25. Ibid., pp. 146f.

26. Ibid., pp. 129, 151.

27. Quoted in ibid., pp. 33f.

28. Ibid., pp. 169f.

29. Ibid., pp. 91f., 150.

30. Ibid., p. 151.

31. Ibid., p. 91.

32. Ibid., p. 151.

33. Ibid., p. 93.

34. Ibid., p. 128; italics added.

35. Ibid., p. 159.

36. Ibid., p. 94.

37. Ibid., p. 48.

38. Ibid., p. 157.

39. Quoted in ibid., p. xv.

40. Ivor Leclerc discusses this development in *The Nature of Physical Existence* (New York: Humanities Press, 1972), Part II, and, briefly, in "The Necessity Today of the Philosophy of Nature," *Process Studies* 3 (Fall 1973): 158ff.

41. See Paul Oestreicher, ed., *The Christian-Marxist Dialogue* (New York: Macmillan, 1969), pp. 140f.

42. A. N. Whitehead, *Modes of Thought* (New York: Free Press, 1968), p. 128.

43. A. N. Whitehead, *Adventures of Ideas* (New York: Free Press, 1967), p. 156.

44. See, e.g., *Adventures of Ideas,* esp. Part II; *Modes of Thought*, ch. 7 and 8; passim in *The Concept of Nature* (Cambridge: Cambridge University Press, 1920); in *An Inquiry Concerning the Principles of Natural Knowledge* (Cambridge: Cambridge University Press, 1919); and in *Science and the Modern World* (New York: Macmillan, 1925).

45. Whitehead, *Modes of Thought*, p. 130.

46. Ibid., p. 138.

47. For an introduction to process philosophy the reader might wish to consult my essay, "The World and God: A Process Perspective," in Norbert O. Schedler, ed., *Philosophy of Religion: Contemporary Perspectives* (New York: Macmillan, 1974), pp. 423–40. Book-length introductions include: Ivor Leclerc, *Whitehead's Metaphysics: An Introductory Exposition* (Bloomington: Indiana University Press, 1975); Victor Lowe, *Understanding Whitehead* (Baltimore: The Johns Hopkins Press, 1962); William A. Christian, *An Interpretation of Whitehead's Metaphysics* (New Haven: Yale University Press, 1959); and, with a different focus, John B. Cobb, Jr., and David Ray Griffin, *Process Theology: An Introductory Exposition* (Philadelphia: Westminster Press, 1976).

48. Even though creativity may not be definable in a strict sense, a greater consensus in its characterization should be possible than now seems to exist in psychological and philosophical analyses. Jeffrey Maitland, a philosopher, apparently takes a contrary viewpoint when he says that "no simple characterization of creativity seems possible" (in "Creativity," *The Journal of Aesthetics and Art Criticism* 34 [Summer 1976]: 407). But Maitland himself very helpfully clarifies the place of

human "foreknowledge" in the creative act, so in this sense a fuller analysis seems entirely possible.

One area of needed clarification suggested by Chapter One of this book is the relationship of creative willing to thinking and feeling. It is impossible to divorce any one of these aspects of selfhood from the others. Thus if we begin with the primacy of the will, as proposed in Chapter One, we shall have to see whether in some way the will cannot be said to "synthesize the cognitive and the affective," as Edna Shapiro suggests (in "Toward a Developmental Perspective on the Creative Process," *Journal of Aesthetic Education* 9 [October 1975]: 72). The work of Silvano Arieti would seem to be especially promising in this regard, in part because it displays a particular affinity to the Whiteheadian conception of selfhood suggested by the argument of this chapter and the previous one. Arieti understands creativity, which he calls the "tertiary process," to be a way of coordinating the affective (the "primary process") and the intellectual (the "secondary process"). This seems strikingly similar to Whitehead's view of the creative activity that constitutes an actual entity, wherein the conceptual prehensions (of the later supplemental phases of concrescence) are derived from, then adjusted, and finally integrated with the physical prehensions (originating in the initial, conformal phase). Those who wish to follow up this apparent parallel will find a thorough description of Whitehead's account of the concrescence of an actual entity (of which a moment of human experience is the paradigm instance) in Donald W. Sherburne, *A Whiteheadian Aesthetic* (New Haven: Yale University Press, 1961), pp. 41–71 (and more briefly in *A Key to Whitehead's Process and Reality* [Bloomington: Indiana University Press, 1966], pp. 36–71). Arieti's position is developed in *American Handbook of Psychiatry* (New York: Basic Books, 1966), Vol. 3, pp. 722–41; in *The Intrapsychic Self* (New York: Basic Books, 1967), part 3; and in *Creativity: The Magic Synthesis* (New York: Basic Books, 1976).

49. The literature on creativity is enormous, even though it is usually spoken of as still very much a developing area of research and reflection. In addition to the works of Arieti, cited above, the reader may wish to consult Harold H. Anderson, ed., *Creativity and Its Cultivation* (New York: Harper, 1959). Anderson's book, containing contributions by Erich Fromm, Rollo May, Carl Rogers, Abraham Maslow, and others, gives the layperson a reasonably broad introduction to various viewpoints on the topic.

50. Recognition of the intentional element in creativity rescues creativity from the fairly common romantic interpretation in which it is viewed as a dimension of the affective mode, a sub-category of feeling. And the intentional character of creativity seems to be widely accepted in both psychology and aesthetic theory. (See Shapiro, "Toward a Developmental Perspective," p. 72, and Maitland, "Creativity," p. 399).

51. This judgment is supported by the study of artistic forms of creativity where one would be most tempted virtually to equate creativity and originality. See, e.g., Maitland, "Creativity," pp. 407f., and Arieti, *Intrapsychic Self*, pp. 330f.

52. If we follow Whitehead's doctrine, described above, that every actual entity possesses some miniscule measure of self-directedness, we must agree with Harold H. Anderson that in some remote fashion "creativity . . . is found in every living cell" (in Anderson, ed., *Creativity and Its Cultivation* [New York: Harper, 1959], p. xii). Further details of the Whiteheadian or "process" view on this issue

may be gleaned from Charles Hartshorne, *The Logic of Perfection and Other Essays in Neoclassical Metaphysics* (LaSalle, Ill.: Open Court, 1973), ch. 6, 7, and 8, and *Creative Synthesis and Philosophic Method* (LaSalle, Ill.: Open Court, 1970), ch. 1.

53. See Paulo Freire, *Pedagogy of the Oppressed* (New York: Seabury Press, 1970).

54. Rubem Alves, *Tomorrow's Child: Imagination, Creativity, and the Rebirth of Culture* (New York: Harper & Row, 1972), p. 160.

55. A. N. Whitehead, *Adventures of Ideas,* p. 75; for Whitehead's understanding of "adventure," see pp. 258f. and 273–296.

56. Ibid., p. 63. In addition to process thought, Maurice Merleau-Ponty's phenomenology of the "living-body" also overcomes the Cartesian separation of the mind from its body and thus creativity from its context. See especially Merleau-Ponty's *Phenomenology of Perception,* trans. Colin Smith (New York: Humanities Press, 1962), but also *The Structure of Behavior* (Boston: Beacon Press, 1963); *Signs,* trans. Richard C. McCleary (Evanston, Ill.: Northwestern University Press, 1964), and James M. Edie, ed., *The Primacy of Perception,* trans. William Cobb et al. (Evanston, Ill.: Northwestern University Press, 1964).

PART TWO

A Christian Theology for Freedom

Chapter Three

The Lure Toward Freedom: An Understanding of God

Chapter One contended that the unique task of our time is to understand human freedom and to decide its worth. Chapter Two sought to develop an understanding of freedom that is coherent and that does justice to contemporary sensibilities, especially to our sense of being autonomous yet related. Both chapters are preparatory to our major concern, which is to develop an appraisal of the worth of human freedom, so understood, from the standpoint of Christian faith.

Many people view Christianity as an opponent of freedom. They do not deny that Christians sometimes speak and act for freedom, but they do question whether Christians, as such, are entitled to that position. What Christians may proclaim at the top of their voices, these critics contend, is in fact denied at the root of their thinking. This is said particularly in connection with Christian forms of belief in God, which belief surely is fundamental to all else Christians hold to be true. In spite of their coincidence in the lives of some people, belief in the Christian God and the affirmation of human freedom are finally irreconcilable. The Christian's occasional defense of freedom is a fortunate inconsistency; the oppressiveness of Christians throughout history is the more fundamental expression of their faith. This is the charge: Christian faith at its heart harbors an opposition to human freedom.

This charge might be ignored if it were voiced only by those whom we could suspect of being antagonistic in their motivation, but it is not. Some who question the compatibility of traditional faith and freedom are among Christianity's most thoughtful adherents. The Protestant theologian Wolfhart Pannenberg, for example, writes: "If God is understood . . . [as in classical theology], then in fact no human freedom would be possible; and on the other hand the experience of freedom excludes belief in the existence of such a God."[1] Because it is fairly widely believed that the affirmation of human freedom is inimical to traditional Christian thinking about God, and vice versa, we would do well to look at some of the reasons behind this judgment.

The Problem of Freedom and God

The first claim that merits our attention has to do with the status of freedom in Christian theology. Roger Garaudy, a contemporary Marxist,

43

contends that belief in God demeans human freedom because it relegates freedom to a place of unimportance, or worse, in the scheme of things. Men and women are created in the image of God, according to traditional doctrine. This suggests, on the surface, that there is some edifying continuity between human beings and God. In truth, though, the opposite —a pernicious discontinuity—is apparent when Christian teaching is examined more systematically. Being human, Garaudy observes, means being incomplete, being always in the process of self-creation; continuous self-creation is essential to human existence.[2] The God of classical Christianity, by contrast, is finished, lacking in nothing, unchanging, complete, "for it is impossible to conceive of a God who is always in process of making himself."[3] Simply to affirm the reality of such a God is to degrade human nature because, by definition, God is the highest good. In Garaudy's view, then, the inexorable if seldom spoken implication of Christian thought is that humanity, far from imaging or mirroring the highest good, is God's antithesis. Apparently, the only alternative to demeaning the incomplete, dynamic nature of persons is to deny the complete, unchanging Christian God.

It is not easy to dismiss Garaudy's concern. In most traditional theology God is an unchanging, finished reality. This view of God has seemed a necessary corollary to the affirmation of God's perfection, for if something is perfect it is inconceivable that it should change. Why? Because change would evidently make a perfect being either more perfect or less perfect, either of which is inconsistent with the notion of a perfect being. If a being becomes more perfect, then it was not really perfect in its prior state. But neither was it originally perfect if it becomes less so, for a truly perfect being would not be susceptible to such a loss of value. A perfect being cannot change. Nor is there any reason why it should "want" to change. It would already possess everything; there would be no reason for it to change. Thus it is that, in traditional thinking, change has seemed foreign to the nature of God.

It is clear, however, that change pervades the human mode of being. Indeed, if freedom is made central to our concept of being human, it is difficult not to think of change, too, as being *essential* to our humanity. But if so, how can a dynamic, changing human nature be said to image, to mirror the totally unchanging nature of God? It does appear that humanity and divinity are antithetical. And if God is good, what are we to think of ourselves? To those like Garaudy, the prominence of self-deprecation in the history of Christian piety does not seem to be tangential. On the contrary, the demeaning of human nature, and particularly of human freedom, is said to be a strict implication of the Christian view of God.

A second consideration in relating faith to freedom pertains to the function of human freedom in Christian theology. In this connection Garaudy maintains that Christianity dehumanizes persons by circumscribing the role of their freedom. Christianity "takes it for granted," he says, quoting Fr. Gonzalez Ruiz, "that man is a simple executor of plans previously made by God. . . ."[4] This allegation is made even more pointedly by the philosopher Kurt Baier. Christianity, Baier charges, reduces humans "to the level of a gadget, a domestic animal, or perhaps a slave." "The Christian world picture," he continues, "sees man as a creature, a divine artifact, something halfway between a robot (manufactured) and an animal (alive), a homunculus, or perhaps Frankenstein, made in God's laboratory, with a purpose or task assigned by his Maker."[5]

Baier's objection may be stated without his verbal extravagance. He is saying that the function of freedom is trivial, in the Christian view. The proper use of freedom is decided in advance and laid out in divine revelation. Although human freedom allows us to accept or reject the divine plan, the "choice" we make—if we *really* believe the plan to be of God—is hardly a serious one in view of the overwhelmingly negative consequences of "noncompliance." Consider a group of islanders who are free to decide whether or not to say "zonie" on prescribed occasions. Their choice is hardly an open one if disobedience is believed to cause the rebel sooner or later to self-destruct. The choice they make is significant, due to its consequences, but the fact that it is made *in freedom* is not important. Even if the number of prescriptions they could, in theory, accept or reject were greatly increased in number and complexity, it is difficult to see that this would increase the significance of their freedom as such. If eternal happiness were the promised reward for the choice of compliance, the value or worth of freedom itself would not thereby be enhanced, for the value would inhere in the obedience or in the bliss it brings but not in the freedom. Indeed, one wonders why obedience is not simply predetermined, except for the eccentricity of the reigning deity who happens to prefer that obedience be accompanied by freedom even if that freedom is vacuous. The connection between *free* obedience and blissful reward is purely arbitrary. Worth does not inhere in freedom *per se,* it lies in obedience.

The parallel with Christian faith, traditionally interpreted, is obvious. Baier is charging that Christian faith renders human freedom vacuous and valueless. While traditional theology may affirm that God gives us freedom, it so severely restricts the legitimate function of that freedom as to make it a trivial possession.

A third consideration, with a long history in theology, has to do with the difficulty of reconciling human freedom and the usual Christian view of God's foreknowledge. Theologians have assumed that God knows the future and, moreover, that God's knowledge of the future is infallible. God is always right about what will occur, not by an extraordinarily long streak of good luck, but because God cannot—logically cannot—be wrong about the future. Therefore, if God knows that we will perform act A tomorrow, then, because God *cannot* be wrong, it follows that we *cannot* do otherwise than perform act A tomorrow. We *must* do whatever God foreknows; otherwise his foreknowledge would not be infallible. But, if we *must* do what we do, human freedom, in the sense of our being able to do otherwise than we do in the same circumstance, is quite impossible. God's foreknowledge, it would seem, can only be protected by denying altogether that humans are free.[6]

There are replies to this argument, but they seem inescapably problematic. One is to say that God foreknows and thus determines what we shall do, but that God foreknows/determines that we shall do these acts freely. When stated with the precision required, however, this reply is senseless. If in fact I cannot but paint the house tomorrow, what does it mean to add that I must paint it freely? If my painting the house is logically necessary, it cannot be free. To say it is both is like saying something is a "round-square." Nothing meaningful is being said.

The more promising reply is to say that God, being timeless, knows past, present and future "all at once." Strictly speaking, from this point of view God has no *fore*knowledge since this would imply that something is future for God; God has knowledge—all knowledge, or omniscience. This strategy, however, saves human freedom, *if* it does, only by making it worthless. For one thing, our freedom, in this view, would make no difference to what occurs in the future, because that future *really* (i.e., for God) already is. Our freedom, then, is ineffectual. Secondly, though human freedom is saved, it is relatively unreal. Indeed, a chimera of unreality is cast over the whole plane of temporal existence. All that is part and parcel of a freedom experienced amidst the passage of time, e.g., the perplexing alternatives we face, the troubling prospect of failure or the hope of success, the agony of choosing, the unsettled consequences—*all* of these elements essential to our temporal freedom are unreal from God's, and thus from the *true*, vantage point. Thirdly, although one can say "God is timeless, yet knows the temporal world," it is difficult to know what that statement can mean.[7] If, on the one hand, the "timefulness" of human reality is taken into God's timeless knowledge, is temporality not thereby introduced into the divine awareness?[8] If, on the other hand, the temporality of our lives is said to be absent in God's knowledge, is the static replica of our lives that is known to God really *us*?

The effort to preserve the doctrine of human freedom by thinking God's (fore)knowledge to be timeless seems futile. The freedom thereby saved is ineffectual, unreal, and apparently unknown to God. The conclusion reached by Pannenberg, therefore, seems altogether accurate: "The key problems of divine foreknowledge . . . show that in fact there is an antinomy in the attitude adopted by traditional Christian theism to human freedom."[9]

The three considerations we have discussed form a powerful critique of Christianity because they claim to locate a hostility to freedom at the very heart of Christian belief, namely, in the Christian doctrine of God. To turn back these criticisms it will therefore be necessary to examine and perhaps even to reformulate the understanding of God. It is conceivable that such an effort will fail, that Christian faith cannot yield an adequate framework for affirming the worth of human freedom. But the question *is* an open one. Advocates of freedom, we should remember, have not always found it necessary to judge Christian faith negatively. Hegel, the modern philosopher in whose work freedom was of central importance, saw Christianity to be the religion of freedom *par excellence*. [10] Marxists like Roger Garaudy and Ernst Bloch acknowledge that again and again Christian faith has loosed a dynamic for freedom and against oppression that would not be bound by any status quo, political or religious. [11] And partisans of liberation in Latin America today claim to ground their struggle in Christian faith. [12] That so robust a power for freedom should have been conveyed so frequently is significant. It suggests that quite possibly the Christian antipathy toward freedom stems not from the lived faith, but rather from the inadequate categories with which theological reflection has sought to interpret that faith. Quite possibly, Jesus, and the tradition of faith which he creates, *does* "mean freedom." [13] Until the antinomies of faith and freedom are resolved, however, such an assertion is rhetoric, and the legitimacy of the *Christian* defense of freedom is unsupported.

The basic difficulty, we have seen, seems to lie in Christian forms of belief in God. Does the Christian God "mean freedom"? To this topic we now turn our attention.

Aseity and Agape

The decisive knowledge of God for Christian faith is rooted in Jesus Christ. Precisely that revelation in Christ, however, no less than that of the Jewish tradition of which it is said to be a part, attests to the fact that the foundation of the believer's being and doing is God. Hence a Christian theology for freedom must seek its systematic basis in the doctrine of God.

The claim that God is creator is central to the Judeo-Christian perspective. As noted in Chapter One, this claim probably became explicit in the process of defending the supremacy of Yahweh, the God of Israel, as against the other deities of Canaan, and it culminated in Hebrew monotheism. The monotheistic idea of the divine creator also served as the primary device for distinguishing early Christianity from its so-called pagan competitors. The main point of the idea that God created the world was to witness to the unqualified dependability or self-sufficiency of God. This is evident from the texts of the apologists and the early Catholic fathers, but it is also apparent from the fact that God was said to be, though in a sense not always clear, the ground of the *divine* existence as well as that of the world. [14] Contrary to what we might have supposed, then, the doctrine that the world was created out of nothing (*ex nihilo*) intended primarily to speak about God. And what was being said eventually emerged in the Middle Ages as the doctrine of God's *aseity*. [15] In this the religious intuition of God's independence, absoluteness, self-sufficiency, received its ultimate doctrinal expression.

Fundamentally, the doctrine of divine *aseity* (Latin: *a,* from; *se,* itself) affirms, as Karl Barth has said, that "God lives from and by Himself."[16] Its purpose was to say that God's existence and character are invulnerable, that the reality and dependability of God do not depend in any respect upon circumstances beyond God. It arose out of the confidence that God can be and is faithful in the fulfillment of the divine promises. Hence it is not surprising that the divine *aseity* tended to become basic to the attributes of God, the divine essence of which the other attributes were perfections.[17]

With Karl Barth we must regret, however, that eventually "the idea of God's *aseitas* was interpreted, or rather supplanted, by that of *independentia* or *infinitas,* and later by that of the unconditioned or absolute."[18] Quite clearly the biblical God was not thought to be independent, infinite, unconditioned, or absolute in *every* respect. These ideas were "serviceable . . . in their place," as Barth recognizes.[19] But their legitimate place was to witness to the unconditioned nature of the divine existence and character. That God is, and that God is loving—both are unaffected, in any way whatsoever, by any circumstances beyond God. Nothing outside of God can alter the fact of God's existence and the fact of God's perfect love. Whatever else is, God is and is loving in relation to that state of affairs.

Precisely because God is perfect love, however, God is also profoundly and genuinely affected by the world. That, of course, is what we find affirmed in the biblical material. In Genesis God is said to have rejoiced in the goodness of creation and to have regretted creating human beings because of their wickedness. Later Yahweh is often grieved by Israel's unfaithfulness and moved to forgiveness by its repentance. God's openness to the world is also apparent in the New Testament. The believer, for example, is exhorted to pray to or draw near to God, to which God will respond (James 1:5, 4:8); clearly, what the believer does has some effect upon, makes some difference to, God. Thus, although the affirmation that God is in some respects independent and changeless is present in the biblical tradition, so too is the claim that God is affected by the world and is in that sense dependent, conditioned, and related. However "serviceable" are those notions that reflect a confidence in God's steadfast character, they cannot be pushed to the point where they obscure the genuine dependence of God upon the world.

We must even say that God "needs" the world, i.e., that God's dependence upon the world is integral to the divine nature. The conviction that "need" is a sign of weakness and thus an imperfection is rooted deep in Hellenistic sensibilities. These sensibilities entered into Christian theology during its early stages and were of enormous value to it. But just as the biblical vision differs from that of the Hellenist by insisting that in some respects God is related and conditioned, so also it may be constrained to speak in a certain sense of God's need. Just this manner of speaking, it would seem, is required by the confidence that God is loving.

In the divine *aseity*, God chooses the selfhood of love or, more specifically, *agape*. Agape is the selfless giving of the self to another. Thus it contrasts with *eros*, a love that is inspired by the inherent worth of its object, desiring to possess and enjoy that object.[20] *Agape* has its source in the character of the lover, not in the object of love. Thus God's *agape* is grounded in God. It is spontaneous in the sense that it flows from God's *aseity* (cf. Matt. 5:45; 20:1-16), not from the worth of the object (though this does not imply, necessarily, the worthlessness of the object). Yet *agape* is also willed. God's love, as such, is not the consequence of some natural necessity, some inescapable natural bond; it results from God's intention, God's choice. The fact of God's love, then, in no way depends upon or "needs" anything beyond the divine nature. God's love is grounded in God alone.

The absolute independence of the fact of God's love, however, by no means indicates that God is totally independent. On the contrary, the concrete reality of that *agape* that God chooses to be is inherently relational. This is evident throughout the biblical depiction of divine love as expressive, as always taking form vis-à-vis an object. It is especially evident in the incarnation, which for the Christian is the paradigm of *agape* (John 3:16; Rom. 5:8). The incarnation is God's selfless self-giving to and for humanity in the humanity of Jesus. Especially for the Christian, then, the relational character of love is undeniable. Love is a type of relationship. Therefore, in his discussion of "The Being of God as the One Who Loves," Karl Barth can write:

> We must now say that He wills to be ours, and He wills that we should be His. He wills to belong to us and He wills that we should belong to Him. He does not will to be without us, and He does not will that we should be without Him. He wills certainly to be God and He does not will that we should be God. But He does not will to be God for Himself nor as God to be alone with Himself. He wills as God to be for us and with us who are not God. Inasmuch as He is Himself and affirms Himself, . . . He places Himself in this relation to us. He does not will to be Himself in any other way than He is in this relationship.[21]

Now if to love is to be related, then to speak of unrelated love is, at best, to speak of potential love and, at worst, to speak nonsense. In neither case do we refer to the God intended by Christian faith. The Christian God everlastingly chooses the nature of love. God is never merely potential love; God *is* love. And because love is relational, there must always be that to which God is related in love. In this manner God's love entails the fact that there is always a world which God loves. And in this sense we may say that God *needs* a world—i.e., in order that God may be what God chooses to be, which is love. God is (always) love only if there is (always) a world to which God may be related.[22]

To summarize the argument to this point: The *aseity* of a loving God cannot be allowed to obscure God's genuine relatedness to the world.

Although independent, unconditioned, and absolute in existence and character, God, precisely because that character is constituted as *agape,* is also dependent, conditioned, and related in the concreteness of the divine experience. Moreover, because God is *always* self-constituted—is *a se*—as love, and because love requires an object, it follows that God always needs a world in order to love. If there is a God of love, there is something other than God, namely a world.[23] God and world everlastingly coexist.[24]

The nature of the God-world relationship requires one additional clarification. We have acknowledged the necessity of saying that God is dependent, as well as independent, in relation to the world. God's dependence, however, would be empty, a mere fiction, if that upon which God depends, i.e., the world, were in turn entirely dependent upon God. In such a case, God's dependence upon the world would be, finally, the dependence of the divine self upon itself. But as biblical faith knows it, love means the relatedness of selves that are in some respect autonomous, independent of one another. This is illustrated by the relationship of God and Israel in Hosea. God implores Israel to return to faithfulness. Such a plea is farcical if Israel, in the last analysis, possesses no real independence, no real power over against God. God genuinely pleads with Israel to return, as Hosea genuinely seeks the return of his wayward wife, because Israel, like Gomer, enjoys some measure of real power. If this mutual independence opens the participants to suffering as well as joy, in proportion to their sensitivity to the other, it is nonetheless only this kind of relatedness that can be loving at all.

From the Christian standpoint, perhaps, the finest statement of the formal aspects of the relationship of perfected love is the Johannine description of Jesus and God—"I and the Father are one" (John 10:30). This is such a telling description, however, because it presupposes a distinction of autonomous selves, as is evident from the distinction between Jesus' selfhood and authority, on the one hand, and God's, on the other, throughout the Fourth Gospel. (See, e.g., John 5:30: "I can do nothing on my own authority; . . . I seek not my own will but the will of him who sent me.") The unity of love, then, is one achieved in the context of the genuine freedom or autonomy of those who are united.

Our analysis of the divine *aseity* and *agape* has led us to see that the God-world relationship is not one of independence-dependence; it is a relationship of interdependence. More precisely, God and world are each in some respects dependent and independent vis-à-vis the other. We shall briefly consider this structure of relatedness before turning to our next topic.

God is independent and dependent with respect to the world. God is *a se,* God exists "from himself" (as tradition has put it), and God "exists from himself" as *agape.* In existence and in the character of steadfast love, God is totally independent. *That* God is and *who* God is are in no respects affected by the world. In this sense—in being and character—God is the most fully independent reality. Precisely because God does choose the character of *agape*, however, the divine life is intimately related to the temporal process. In the quality of its content the divine life is vulnerable. God's purposes are frustrated or furthered by finite beings, and the finite response makes a difference to the life of God. And because we are led by the biblical witness to say that God's *agape* is "pure, unbounded love," we must say, too, that God knows all there is to know, enjoys all there is to enjoy, and suffers all there is to suffer. In this sense—in the content of the divine life—God is the most fully dependent reality.

The world is dependent and independent with respect to God. We have seen that God cannot be dependent upon the world in any real sense if the world is wholly dependent upon God. The world's partial autonomy is implicit in the belief that the cosmic process makes a genuine difference to God. Because the world is something other than God, it can in some measure enrich or impoverish the quality of God's experience. The world has some independence. Quite obviously, however, the biblical witness attests to a cosmic dependence upon God. God is creator-redeemer. God is that reality which brings the world from chaos to life. We shall see shortly how thoroughly partisan this makes God, how righteous is God's love. For now we may simply observe that the world depends upon God as the supreme agent of right-making in the temporal process: "Thus says God, the Lord, who created the heavens and ... spread forth the earth ... : 'I am the Lord, I have called you to righteousness ... to open the eyes that are blind, to bring out the prisoners from the dungeon, from the prison those who sit in darkness' "(Isa. 42:5–7).

The Freedom of God

The parallel between the preceding description of the Christian God and our earlier characterization of freedom is obvious. The poles of freedom, we said in Chapter Two, are creativity and contextuality. Each alone is an abstraction. Together they constitute freedom. Freedom is creativeness, a "coming from oneself," that occurs within a conditioning context, a context that enriches or impoverishes, encourages or inhibits, but does not determine.

God is free because God is contextual creativity. If creativity is an intentional spontaneity grounded finally in itself, God's *aseity* is the supreme instance of creativity, for God's reality and character are rooted in the infinite potentiality of the divine reality. If contextuality is openness to surrounding circumstance, God's relatedness is the supreme instance of contextuality, for God opens the divine life to the full concreteness of the entire temporal order. No being is more independent and more dependent, more absolute and more relative, more creative and more contextual. No being is more free. And no being *can* be more free. In no other experience can the world be more fully and vividly ingredient, for no experience can be more inclusive than pure *agape*. In no other experience can the contextual data be more creatively taken into itself, for no experience can be more autonomous than pure *aseity*. God is unsurpassable freedom. Such is the logic of the Christian witness.

The nature of God's freedom for Christian faith may be clarified in relation to the divine love, the divine evaluation, and the divine power.

GOD'S FREEDOM AND LOVE

The divine metaphysical essence is *aseity*. This is God's necessary characteristic, that which God must be. We may even say, with Sartre and Whitehead, that all persons are necessarily self-creative, or, with Whitehead, that all actual entities at whatever level are self-creative in some degree. In either case we should have to acknowledge, however, that the exercise of creativity is frequently meager, restricted in the resources of possibility and actuality, and thus deficient in vigor. Usually it is a task betrayed, as we shall have occasion to discuss later. But *aseity*, which may in some sense be called the essence of all that is actual, is in God fully realized. One of the meanings of divine perfection is the unrestrictedness of that creativity which grounds God's own life in itself and brings forth a world from chaos.

We said in Chapter Two that creativity is an abstraction in the sense that we cannot conceive of a creativity that is devoid of some context. It would seem on purely logical grounds, then, that God's *aseity*, being the supreme instance of creativity, must also be contextual. But whatever the purely logical conclusion, we are surely led to this conclusion from within the standpoint of faith, for the Christian God chooses to love. If God's metaphysical essence is *aseity*, *agape* is God's volitional essence. Love is that nature the divine nature chooses for itself. Hence we could not agree with Karl Barth that "God's love is necessary," if the necessity in question were metaphysical.[25]

There is no contradiction involved in thinking of a being identical in every respect to the God of Christian faith, except for the momentous difference that this being chooses to love less. Such a being would still be related to the world to the degree that its creativity requires some context. But the degree of relatedness entered into would merely be that which serves the narrower interests of the "lover." In this instance, love would not be *agape* and the being in question would not be the Christian God, not a God worthy of worship and gratitude, not a God of grace and righteousness. But precisely because God's love is not necessary, yet offered without fail, we may speak of the divine faithfulness. Faithfulness is possible only where it is contingent.[26] We affirm the faithfulness of God because God's steadfast love is rooted in the divine *aseity*, because in freedom God chooses to be *agape*.

God's love, God's self-giving, is affirmation. It is the affirmation, first, of contextuality. It is the affirmation of dependence, of indebtedness. God's love is a willingness to abandon the protection of relative isolation for the risk of relatedness. It is a grace in the universe that accepts fully and unreservedly a relatedness to the world that might have been circumscribed. Grace is that divine love which affirms the entire created order as the proper context of the divine becoming.

But love must not be viewed as pure acceptance, pure affirmation, pure "togetherness." Love is the acceptance of creativity no less than of contextuality, for in freedom God chooses to love freedom—context *and* creativity. God's love, therefore, is a commitment to the sustenance and enhancement of finite creativity, to the capacity of each creature to "come from itself" in a rich, ennobling context. In the words of Genesis 2, cited in Chapter One, love calls each creature to "name" itself, and to "name" the orders of freedom. Conversely, then, divine love opposes everything in persons and structures that inhibits creativity. Love opposes, disrupts, and seeks to destroy all that opposes, disrupts, and seeks to destroy the capacity of creatures to "come from themselves." If it must, love brings "not . . . peace, but a sword" (Matt. 10:34). Still, love has no basis for cherishing its own freedom more dearly than that of another. Love "seeks not its own" (1 Cor. 13:5). Thus the sword of love may well seek *self*-sacrifice, believing that sometimes the sacrifice of one's own freedom best serves the freedom of all. Love judges. Judgment is that divine love in the world which loosens and holds, shatters and sustains, opposes and protects, damns and preserves, and shares fully the pain of the ones judged, even while it is the one who judges.

GOD'S FREEDOM AND VALUE

To value, we said in Chapter Two, is to grade something, to order or rank it in relation to other things. To value is to evaluate, and all value refers to the activity of some subject of experience.[27] We have already proposed that *aseity* be viewed as characteristic of all that is actual, at least in the sense that we have used the term. If this position is not required by Christian faith, it is surely allowed. It is an extension of the doctrine of *imago dei,* holding that every level of creation, and not simply the human level, images or mirrors God's nature in some appropriate degree. Assuming this perspective, we may say that all actuality is evaluative.[28]

This doctrine may be expressed in Whiteheadian terms by saying that each actual entity, each fundamental unit of actuality, is a coming together of influences, of evaluations, derived from the distant and immediate past that forms its context. The achievement of each such moment or entity is a synthesis of these influences. That synthesis renders some streams of influence to be of central importance, some of less importance, and some are rendered trivial, data "entertained" in a merely formal fashion only to be dismissed into irrelevance. The criterion of each such synthesis is the controlling purpose, the "subjective aim," as Whitehead calls it, of the becoming occasion. The origins of that aim, among others, lie outside of that entity, as we shall see, but the evolution of that subjective aim toward specificity, and its adoption, are grounded in the becoming occasion itself. Thus the synthesis is, finally, the creative achievement of that becoming occasion. It is that actual entity's creativity. And creativity is, in one of its aspects, evaluation; it is a grading of the elements in the datum, including evaluations inherited from the past, in terms of its selected purpose or subjective aim. Any given moment of human experience is an instance of synthetic creativity, as is any given actual entity constituting one of the subatomic processes of nature. The quality and richness of creativity varies almost infinitely from subatomic events through higher forms of nature and human life to the life of God. But each unit of actuality is creative in some degree, each is *a se*. Thus all actuality is evaluative.

A divine love that cherishes creativity cherishes, too, the evaluative function of creativity. We must therefore say, as a beginning, that God values valuing as such. But just as love is not indifferent acceptance, so God's cherishing of valuation is not indifferent. Certain structures, in the very nature of the case, contribute to the preservation of freedom, namely those that enhance creativity and enrich its context. No one, not even God, decides whether freedom will flourish in the mediocrity of one-dimensional abundance, in the rootless pursuit of novelty for its own sake, in the structural deprivation of racism and sexism, in hunger and disease. God does not decide the requisites of freedom.[29] In freedom God decides *for* freedom. Hence God cherishes those finite evaluations that sustain and enhance the capacity of creative evaluation at every level of the temporal process.

GOD'S FREEDOM AND POWER

God and the world constitute a community of essentially free beings (however distorted that essential nature may be), and thus an evaluative community. God's freedom, and consequently God's evaluation, is in some sense one among many. It always coexists "alongside" a world, with no guarantee that it is evident in the world or that it will be conformed to. There can be no assurance of conformity, for the divine evaluation coexists with and seeks to preserve a cosmic community of freedom. The divine purpose to recall finite entities to the realization of their essential freedom could not be imposed, were that even possible, without defeating itself.[30] The very freedom God nurtures disallows in principle any assurance of conformity to God's aims on behalf of freedom. What then *can* God do? What is the nature and extent of God's power?

Christian theologians have traditionally affirmed that the doctrine of God's love entails the limitedness of the divine power in the world. They have usually added, though, that this limitation is self-imposed and that potentially (i.e., apart from the divine self-limitation) God's power is absolute. The reasons for maintaining the doctrine of God's omnipotence are in large measure historical, one would think. In human affairs there is, or seems to be, a correlation between a ruler's increase in power and an increase in that ruler's capacity to accomplish her or his purposes. We today may find—perhaps because we want desperately to find—contrary evidence, as in the case of the totalitarian regime whose excessive power seems to bring about its own dissolution. But the evidence for this judgment of ours is not clear, and it would probably be less clear where the presumption of the right to freedom—a very modern notion, after all—is not given at least lip service. The assumption of a correlation between the degree of power and the capacity of a being to accomplish its purposes has therefore seemed reasonable. Consequently, however resolutely traditional Christian thinkers have retained the doctrine of the limitation of power implicit in divine love, they have also felt constrained by their experience of effective governance to hold for God in reserve, as it were, the capacity to exercise unlimited or absolute power. To do this they have said that God's limitedness is self-imposed—God limits, and therefore can "unlimit," the divine power.

Whatever the historical background, there are difficulties with this way of viewing God's power, from a Christian standpoint. First, if God's love entails that there always be a partially autonomous world, as we have argued, then the divine power over the world is *in fact always* limited, regardless of the alternatives that might be merely conceivable. In fact, God's absolute power never was, is, or will be actualized; it is always delimited by the love God has for the world. For a God of love, omnipotence is an empty possibility at best. But it is also true, in the second place, that for Christian faith an absolutely powerful being *who is truly God* is not even possible; it is, in the strict sense, inconceivable. Christian faith maintains, as we have seen, that the greatest conceivable power, morally speaking, is that of a loving God whose power is limited, even if self-limited, vis-à-vis the world. Absolute or unlimited power is not the greatest conceivable power. But God, of course, is defined as the greatest conceivable being. From this it follows that God cannot be, or even seek to be, absolute or unlimited power, for to say that the greatest conceivable being possesses, or even seeks to possess, a power which is in any way less-then-the-greatest conceivable is a contradiction. Put differently, from the standpoint of *Christian* sensibilities, "absolute power" is not a "perfection" and thus can in no conceivable circumstance be attributed to that being who is truly God.[31]

If the preceding reflections are correct, it is not surprising that A. N. Whitehead said he found the model for his notion of supreme persuasive power in what he calls the "brief Galilean vision."[32] Plato, Whitehead says, had earlier seen that "the divine element in the world is to be conceived as a persuasive agency and not as a coercive agency," but Plato failed to integrate this insight into the rest of his theory.[33] "Can there be any doubt," Whitehead asks, "that the power of Christianity lies in its revelation in act, of that which Plato divined in theory?"[34]

In the understanding of the Christian view of God here developed,

God is the supreme power—the supreme power for freedom—in the universe. At the initiation of each becoming occasion of experience, human and nonhuman, God's evaluation for that becoming event is present as one datum among others in its inheritance. Whitehead calls this divine evaluation the "ideal aim," and he relates it to the appeal of conscience in our moral experience. The ideal aim is that which God deems to be most consonant with the requirements of richness and spontaneity in that becoming occasion, i.e., the requirements for the strengthening of freedom. The power of the divine ideal is its own intrinsic worth. Its efficacy is persuasive, not coercive. And the supremacy of the divine power is its pervasiveness. No moment of becoming escapes the beckoning "oughtness" of the divine evaluation. The finite occasions, in their own freedom, may replace the divine call to observe the requirements of freedom with divergent "oughtnesses" of their own making, with alternative evaluations, thus weakening freedom. Some, like a Job, may challenge the judgment of the supreme power, and thus call into question its "Godliness." Such a morally based rebellion, against God on behalf of freedom, is possible. But the witness of faith's hard experience is that the Jobs, however notable for their moral seriousness, are wrong, that God's will is always faithful to freedom. The supreme power in the universe has, in freedom, chosen freedom. By virtue of its faithfulness and universal presence, the divine being is the ground of that resistible but unwavering lure toward freedom that will not let us go.

God and Human Freedom Reconsidered

At the beginning of this chapter we considered three arguments which maintained that the Christian understanding of God masks a fundamental hostility to freedom. It is now possible, as a conclusion, to reconsider these arguments.

The first contention was that the doctrine of God in Christianity demeans human freedom. A static, changeless divine nature, and a dynamic, changing human nature are opposites. If the divine nature is said to be good, essential human nature is not. Far from mirroring or imaging the nature of God, human nature, and especially human freedom, is its antithesis.

A theology faithful to the biblical understanding of God, however, must emphatically reject the notion of a fixed, unchanging deity. This idea was always troublesome to theologians because it was clearly at variance with the experience of faith. Still, for long periods of Western history conceptualities which favored independence, changelessness, etc., seemed to be the most adequate ones available. In such conceptual systems the notion of a fixed, static being epitomized perfection. The modes of thought by which we seek understanding today, however, center upon interdependence and process. Without finality for our present ways of thinking, and without supposing that the past has nothing left to teach us

we may nevertheless acknowledge that processive and relational conceptualities seem to us today to be the most adequate ones, logically and
experientially, in science, aesthetics, psychology, ethics, etc. Certainly
these categories, which in an important sense may have derived from the
biblical worldview, seem to be the most adequate vehicles for expressing
the Christian view of God.

A God who is *a se* cannot but be viewed as a dynamic, free reality.
Indeed, we may say, with Karl Barth, for example, that the essence of God
is freedom.[35] And just as we find human freedom to be characterized by
creativity and contextuality, so also God's. God is creative. Yet the divine
creativity, no less than ours, is rooted in God's relatedness to a world, a
context. The God who is essentially free cannot be an aloof, self-
contained, totally self-sufficient being. The notion of "absolute freedom"
is no less nonsensical with reference to divinity than humanity. Any being,
including God, is essentially related to a world and dependent in some
measure upon it. The Hebrew-Christian God affirms that relatedness and
perfects it. God is the supreme instance of freedom—creativity and contextuality. If the dynamic, related God of freedom is indeed the highest
good, as faith affirms, then our essential human nature is scarcely demeaned. In fact, on this view, human freedom *does* image or mirror the
nature of God.

The second argument amounts to the claim that the existence of a God
of right and power trivializes human freedom. If God defines the right
and good, what have we to decide? If, through the threat of eternal
damnation, God enforces the divine preferences, again, what real decision is left to human freedom? And what similarity is there between divine
creativity, the source of right and value, and human creativity, whose only
rational function is compliance? Freedom's choice is "to obey or not to
obey," which, given the threat of righteous damnation, is no choice at all.

The answer available to Christian thought is not, I think, to minimize
the threat of lostness, nor is it to neutralize divine power. There is much
that is abhorrent in traditional Christian talk of heaven, hell, eternal
judgment, etc., and much that is not abhorrent is pathetically self-
centered. But there is more. The varied symbols of eternal salvation and
damnation in Christian theology wisely attest to the fact that, even in
purely "secular" terms, there is genuine and irretrievable lostness in the
temporal process. Forms of Christianity that minimize lostness take on the
cast of an optimism refuted by our experience. Life has its tragedy that no
future can undo. All is not saved; some things are lost.

It is important to see, however, that the reality of lostness is not
grounded in the arbitrary whim of a deity who could have had it otherwise. The losses of freedom are rooted in the requisites of freedom and
the unrepeatability of time, both matters of metaphysical necessity. Freedom neglected or prevented is freedom lost forever. It is irretrievable, not
because some regnant deity, miffed at human insolence, wills or even

permits its loss, but because a freedom missed for whatever reason is an unactualized freedom, and a freedom that is never actual, is not. No reality, not even God, can save that which is not. The nature of the future of freedom must be clarified in the last chapter of this book. For now we must recognize, however, that we do not elevate freedom by minimizing its negative potentialities.

Neither can we elevate freedom's importance by neutralizing God's power. God does not, and cannot, possess all-power, we have argued. But God is supremely powerful and supremely partisan. Relentlessly seeking the realization of divinely elected purposes, God urges the world toward the fullness of freedom. Sometimes—often, it seems—the divine lure is frustrated. The heart cries, "How long, O God, is the foe to scoff?" (Psalms 74:10). At other times we, like the people of Israel content in their Egyptian captivity, are shaken from bondage and moved toward freedom when we neither want nor expect it. God takes sides, tempting, pleading, assaulting us in our freedom, on behalf of freedom.

However, God's evaluations do not render ours impotent or insignificant. The creative venture is a risk for God. The victories of God's purposes are rooted in the divine persistence, in the compelling worth of the divine ideals, and in the free creaturely response. But God's evaluations do not enjoy privileged status, ontologically. They are not imposed by God. Neither are they established "in the nature of things." The divine evaluations have the same ontological status as do our own commitments and evaluations. In addition, God's evaluations do not "trivialize" our own. There is no reason to speak of a single divine will, except in the general sense of the will to freedom. God does not will our lives. There are many forms of freedom, and many paths to each. Our freedom is manifest in our decisions to advocate or to obstruct freedom, to be sure, but it is also expressed in our creative exploration of freedom's manifold possibilities. God does not will our lives; God wills that we, caring for freedom, use our freedom to "name" the forms of freedom in which to dwell.

The third argument against faith on behalf of freedom points up the incompatibility between God's foreknowledge, traditionally conceived, and human freedom. If God infallibly knows the future, the future cannot be other than God knows it to be. The future is not really open, although it may appear to us to be, and human freedom (if the notion is to be employed at all) is not effectual, real, or known to God.

A theology faithful to freedom must stand by the doctrine of an open future. The future is as yet partially indeterminate; things are yet to be decided. And because of this, time is linear, it enters into novelty. Time is genuinely cumulative. Each new present moment adds something to the temporal process that is not simply an extrapolation from the past. It is the presence of freedom in time that takes time somewhere new, as we might say. Freedom makes the future open. And it is freedom that transforms the indeterminacy, the openness, into determinacies that are better or worse.

A being who is all-knowing will know all things as they are—the actual as actual and the possible as possible.[36] If the temporal process of nature and history is determinate in its pastness, and partially indeterminate in its future, it will be known as such by one whose knowledge is perfect. God does know perfectly. God knows all—the past as past (determinate actuality) and the future as future (partially indeterminate possibility). But God does not know as actual what is possible or as possible what is actual. An omniscient God knows the future as it is—as partially open, with risks and opportunities. An omniscient God of freedom, the God of Christian faith, accepts these risks, seeking in them opportunity for the advancement of freedom.

The present doctrine of God's knowledge parallels in an interesting way the traditional understanding of God's power. In the traditional view, God chooses the risks of self-limited power in order that finite freedom might be real; had God cared less for freedom, God could have avoided the risk of limitedness. Similarly in our view with respect to God's knowledge, God could have avoided the significant risks of an open future by allowing the cosmic process to remain at its lowest, machinelike levels where freedom is mere potency, a peripheral abstraction. In this kind of world, the potentialities of the future would have been severely restricted. The future would have been virtually certain, and God's inferential knowledge of the future sure in every important detail. No risks, no surprises, and no significant realization of possibility. But God, accepting a far more limited grasp of the future, chose to lure the world toward the fulfillment of freedom. To the God of the Christian witness, the possibilities of freedom are worth the relative uncertainty and the risks entailed by an open future.

Notes

1. Wolfhart Pannenberg, *The Idea of God and Human Freedom* (Philadelphia: Westminster Press), p. 93.

2. See Roger Garaudy, *From Anathema to Dialogue* (New York: Herder and Herder, 1966), pp. 74f., and "Creative Freedom" in Paul Oestreicher, ed., *The Christian-Marxist Dialogue* (New York: Macmillan, 1969), pp. 147–64.

3. Garaudy, *Anathema,* p. 95.

4. Ibid., p. 33; cf. "God is alienating in so far as he is regarded as a Moral Law existing before the creation of man, as a heteronomy, opposed to the autonomy of man," in Oestreicher, ed., *Christian-Marxist Dialogue,* p. 144.

5. Kurt Baier, "The Meaning of Life," in M. Weitz, ed., *Twentieth Century Philosophy: The Analytic Tradition* (New York: Free Press, 1966), p. 367. See, too, Erich Fromm, *Man For Himself* (New York: Holt, Rinehart & Winston, 1947), pp. 12f., 143ff.

6. For a thorough defense of this argument, see Nelson Pike, "Divine Omniscience and Voluntary Action," *Philosophical Review* 74 (January 1965): 27–46; cf. also Pike's book, *God and Timelessness* (New York: Schocken, 1970). Charles Hartshorne takes a similar position; see the references below in note 36.

7. It is sometimes argued that God knows about sin without being sinful; therefore, in an analogous way, God can know about time without being temporal. In response we should observe, first, that if sin is viewed as the perverse use of freedom, it is difficult to know how God *can* know about sin unless God is free; and freedom, it would seem, inescapably involves temporal succession. If so, the first side of the alleged analogy can be developed only by presupposing that there is temporal succession in God. But even if, for the sake of argument, we suppose that a wholly nontemporal God does possess a knowledge of sin, it remains doubtful that the analogy drawn between God's knowledge of sin and of temporality is a proper one. Sin is a perverse qualification of an attribute, freedom, which God too possesses. Temporality, by contrast, is not the modification of some divine attribute, such as God's eternality; thus, even an inferential knowledge of temporality seems impossible for a wholly timeless God.

8. The ramifications of this are brought out more fully in Norman Kretzmann, "Omniscience and Immutability," *The Journal of Philosophy* 63 (July 14, 1966): 409–21. See also Charles Hartshorne, *The Divine Relativity: A Social Conception of God* (New Haven: Yale University Press, 1948), ch. 3.

9. Pannenberg, *Idea of God and Human Freedom*, p. 107.

10. Cf. Peter Hodgson, *New Birth of Freedom: A Theology of Bondage and Liberation* (Philadelphia: Fortress Press, 1976), p. 42.

11. See Garaudy, *From Anathema to Dialogue*, pp. 111–119; Ernst Bloch, *Atheism in Christianity* (New York: Herder and Herder, 1972).

12. See, e.g., Rubem A. Alves, *A Theology of Human Hope* (St. Meinrad, Ind.: Abbey Press, 1974); Gustavo Gutiérrez, *A Theology of Liberation* (Maryknoll, N.Y.: Orbis Books, 1973). The following books provide good historical introductions to liberation theology: José Míguez Bonino, *Doing Theology in a Revolutionary Situation* (Philadelphia: Fortress Press, 1974); Enrique Dussel, *History and the Theology of Liberation* (Maryknoll, N.Y.: Orbis Books, 1976), and *Ethics and the Theology of Liberation* (Maryknoll, N.Y.: Orbis Books, 1978), and Robert McAfee Brown, *Theology in a New Key* (Philadelphia: Westminster Press, 1978). Among the numerous introductory essays and articles are Gustavo Gutiérrez, "Freedom and Salvation: A Political Problem," in G. Gutíerrez and R. Shaull, *Liberation and Change* (Atlanta: John Knox Press, 1977); Gustavo Gutiérrez-Merino, "Liberation Movements and Theology," in Edward Schillebeeckx and Bas van Iersel, eds., *Jesus Christ and Human Freedom*, Concilium 93 (New York: Herder and Herder, 1974), pp. 135–46, and Raúl Vidales, "Some Recent Publications in Latin America on the Theology of Liberation," in Claude Geffré and Gustavo Gutiérrez, eds., *The Mystical and Political Dimension of the Christian Faith*, Concilium 96 (New York: Herder and Herder, 1974), pp. 127–36.

13. *Jesus Means Freedom* is the title of a book by Ernst Käsemann (Philadelphia: Fortress Press, 1970).

14. On this development see J. N. D. Kelly, *Early Christian Doctrines* (New York: Harper, 1958), pp. 83–87, and H. A. Wolfson, *The Philosophy of the Church Fathers* (Cambridge: Harvard University Press, 1956), pp. 89f.

15. A. E. Breen, "Aseity," in *The Catholic Encyclopedia* (New York: Robert Appleton Co., 1907), Vol. 1, p. 774.

16. Karl Barth, *Church Dogmatics* (Edinburgh: T. & T. Clark, 1957), Vol. 2, 1, p. 272.

17. James J. Fox, "Attributes, Divine," in *The Catholic Encyclopedia,* Vol. 2, pp. 63f.

18. Barth, *Church Dogmatics,* II, 1, p. 303.

19. Ibid.

20. Anders Nygren, whose *Agape and Eros* (Philadelphia: Westminster Press, 1953) is perhaps the modern classic on the Christian view of love, contrasts the two absolutely, an interpretation that is widely regarded as being too extreme. That there are fundamental differences between *agape* and *eros,* however, is not denied.

21. Barth, *Church Dogmatics,* II, 1, p. 274.

22. It might be said that a solitary God could nevertheless be loving in the Christian view, in as much as love could exist between the "persons" of the Trinity. The problem with this proposal is that it distorts the meaning of "person" in traditional Trinitarian reflection. As Van A. Harvey points out, ". . . no important Christian theologian has argued that there are three self-conscious beings in the godhead. On the contrary, Augustine's favorite analogy for the triune god was one self-consciousness with its three distinctions of intellect, will, and the bond between them." (See Harvey's *A Handbook of Theological Terms* [New York: Macmillan, 1964], p. 246.) One might say, of course, that God is characterized by a type of internal relatedness, but the single, internally related diety is not thereby shown to be related to anything beyond itself. The only form of love a solitary Trinitarian God could manifest is *self*-love, much as a solitary human self could be said to love its body, its career, or its mind. Self-love is in some respects appropriate for humans, no doubt, and it is certainly characteristic of the Aristotelian God. But self-love is not the decisive characteristic of the God of the biblical vision, whose love is said to be *agape,* a selfless giving of the self to another self.

23. I have tried to show on strictly Christian grounds that God must be viewed as absolute, etc., in some respects, and relative, etc., in others, and thus that God and world coexist. The metaphysical perspective of A. N. Whitehead, I should add, allows us to give coherent expression to this understanding of God. But it is undoubtedly Charles Hartshorne who, more than anyone else, has worked out its details. The best introduction to Hartshorne's work in this area is probably *The Divine Relativity* (cited earlier), and *Man's Vision of God and the Logic of Theism* (Chicago: Willett, Clark & Co., 1941). Hartshorne's most recent philosophical work is *Creative Synthesis and Philosophic Method* (LaSalle, Ill.: Open Court, 1970).

24. We need not say that *this* world, this cosmic order or epoch, has always coexisted with God, of course, but only that some world or other always stands in relationship to God. The present cosmological order may have been preceded by an epoch of relative chaos, compared to the present, and that by other epochs or "worlds" of less or more order. This view is entirely faithful to the Judeo-Christian understanding of creation, I believe, and even to the meaning of the Genesis myth, which clearly does not require the doctrine that this world was created *ex nihilo,* as Old Testament scholars have long recognized.

25. Barth, *Church Dogmatics,* II, I, p. 280. Barth did *not* intend to speak of metaphysical necessity, of course, studiously avoiding, as he did, all "natural theology." The necessity he affirms is a necessity of faith, i.e., divine love is necessary in order that God be God.

26. I have discussed this topic more fully (and technically) in "Freedom and Faithfulness in Whitehead's God," *Process Studies* 2 (Summer 1972): 137–48.

27. It is interesting that this analysis of value finds support not only in the traditions of existentialism (Nietzsche and Sartre) and process philosophy (Whitehead), as pointed out in Chapter 2, but also in the work of the analytic philosopher, J. O. Urmson. See Urmson's essay, "On Grading," in *Mind* 59 (1950): 145–59.

28. This doctrine, we said in the second chapter, makes it possible to relate human evaluations to a broader context, one that is natural as well as divine, in that way overcoming Sartre's apparent arbitrariness. The philosophical merit of this view is widely defended in process literature as the solution to that entire complex of modern philosophical problems stemming from Descartes' dualism. See, e.g., Ivor Leclerc, *Whitehead's Metaphysics: An Introductory Exposition* (London: Allen and Unwin, 1958), esp. pp. 124ff.; John B. Cobb, Jr., *A Christian Natural Theology* (Philadelphia: Westminster Press, 1965), pp. 23ff.; Charles Hartshorne, *Reality as Social Process* (Boston: Beacon Press, 1953), ch. 1; and Hartshorne, *Creative Synthesis and Philosophic Method,* ch. 1.

29. On the claim that metaphysical principles are "beyond divine decision," see David Ray Griffin, *God, Power, and Evil: A Process Theodicy* (Philadelphia: Westminster Press, 1976), pp. 297–300.

30. J. L. Mackie, Antony Flew, and others have argued that God could have constituted human beings so that they would freely always choose the good (in our terms, choose in accord with the requisites of freedom). This argument is sound, however, only if one assumes, as they do, a "soft-determinist" view of freedom. The soft-determinist holds that one is free, even if determined, so long as the determinants are internal constraints, such as one's character, and not external constraints, such as a gun, physical force, and the like. But since, for the soft-determinist, the internal constraints are themselves entirely determined, finally, by external circumstances, this view of freedom differs fundamentally from the existentialist, Whiteheadian, and classical "libertarian" view operative in the present work. Given our understanding of freedom, the argument of Flew and Mackie is not compelling. (See Antony Flew, "Divine Omnipotence and Human Freedom" in A. Flew and A. MacIntyre, eds., *New Essays in Philosophical Theology* [London: SCM Press, 1955], pp. 144–69, and J. L. Mackie, "Evil and Omnipotence," *Mind* 54 [1955]: 200–212).

31. For many years Charles Hartshorne has argued (convincingly, to my mind) that from *any* standpoint, Christian or otherwise, the concept of unlimited power or omnipotence ("all-power") is meaningless, except in a strictly monistic universe. In *The Divine Relativity* Hartshorne writes: "The notion of a cosmic power that determines all decisions fails to make sense. For its decisions could refer to nothing except themselves. They could result in no world; for a world must consist of local agents making their own decisions. Instead of saying that God's power is limited, suggesting that it is less than some conceivable power, we should rather say: his power is absolutely maximal, the greatest power, but even the greatest possible power is still one power among others, is not the only power" (p. 138, cf. pp. 134–42). Hartshorne's arguments are clearly and systematically summarized by David R. Griffin in *God, Power, and Evil,* pp. 266–74.

32. A. N. Whitehead, *Process and Reality* (New York: Macmillan, 1929), p. 520.

33. A. N. Whitehead, *Adventures of Ideas* (New York: Free Press, 1967), p. 166.

34. Ibid., p. 167.

35. "By freedom," Barth writes, "we denote what was called in the theology of the Early Church the *aseitas Dei*" (*Church Dogmatics,* II, 1, p. 302). Actually, our own use of the term "freedom" is broader than Barth's; we have included in the term, and thus in God's essence, the divine relatedness (which Barth by no means denies to God) no less than the divine creativity or *aseity.*

36. Charles Hartshorne is the person who has most vigorously and persuasively developed this view of omniscience. See *The Divine Relativity,* pp. 6–18, 116–24; *Man's Vision of God,* pp. 98ff., and passim; and Hartshorne's entries on "omniscience" and "foreknowledge" in Vergilius Ferm, ed., *An Encyclopedia of Religion* (New York: Philosophical Library, 1945).

Chapter Four

The Denial of Freedom: An Understanding of Sin

If some persons doubt the compatibility of the Christian's God and freedom's worth, others find the Christian doctrine of sin to be especially inimical to the affirmation of freedom. This seems particularly true of believers. Human freedom would have been supremely worthwhile in a state of innocence, the traditional Christian will acknowledge, but in the present state of human corruption the rights and possibility of freedom have been forfeited. True freedom in our present condition is freedom from our natural freedom, if it is anything at all. Because it is corrupt, the exercise of that freedom which we have in common as persons is in fact sin. Obedience and bondage, not the practice of freedom, are the ideals of Christian existence, in this view.

Although obedience, bondage, and the corruption of freedom are all themes intrinsic to Christian faith, the Christian doctrine of sin, I shall maintain in this chapter, presupposes the continuing possibility and worth of our common human freedom. Sin is precisely that denial of freedom which Christians so often mistakenly believe to be a virtue. In order to make this point, we shall look at the traditional doctrine of sin, seeing how it comes to expression in a Christian theology for freedom.

The Situation of Sin: Anxiety

We may begin by considering the situation of sin, the condition in which sin is said to arise, in a Christian analysis. Christian theology has generally been at pains not to equate human existence, as such, with sinfulness, because, for one thing, such an equation would remove from human beings the responsibility for sin. The strategy has been to locate in human existence that which is the occasion of sin without claiming that this condition is sin's cause. The condition of sin in the myth of the Fall (Gen. 3) is said to be temptation. There is an inclination not to accept this as the full story, however, since this account leaves unanswered the question, why is X (the forbidden tree, in the myth) a temptation? There-fore, as regularly and reasonably as biblical analyses insist upon an objec-tive, external element in temptation (usually in the form of Satan), there is also the recognition that what renders temptation tempting lies within. The Epistle of James says: "Each person is tempted . . . by his own desire"

64

(1:14), thus placing the fundamental condition of sin within the structure of the self.

Christian theology has analyzed this internal condition of sin in several ways, but the category of "anxiety," particularly as it has come to expression in the work of Reinhold Niebuhr, probably best sums up the thrust of these analyses. "What is the situation," Niebuhr asks, "which is the occasion of temptation?"[1] By way of an answer Niebuhr describes human existence "at the juncture of nature and spirit." Here, he says, we are "both free and bound, both limited and limitless." "Like the animals [we are] involved in the necessities and contingencies of nature; but unlike the animals [we see] this situation and anticipate its perils." Further, we contemplate the vast range of our "seemingly limitless possibilities" and are disturbed by our ignorance of their true boundaries. Thus we are anxious, prone to want to escape into the security of either pure freedom or pure necessity. "Anxiety is the inevitable concomitant of the paradox of freedom and finiteness . . . , the inevitable spiritual state" of our lives. Still, Niebuhr insists that anxiety "not be identified with sin because there is always the ideal possibility that . . . faith in the ultimate security of God's love would overcome all immediate insecurities in nature and history." Hence Jesus coupled his injunction "Do not be anxious" with the assurance that "your heavenly Father knows that you need these things" (Matt. 6:31–32). Anxiety, then, "must be distinguished from sin . . . because it is its precondition and not its actuality."

Niebuhr's treatment of anxiety does not summarize explicit orthodox teaching, of course, partly because traditional belief has been fragmentary in this area, and partly because Niebuhr's exposition draws heavily from existentialist presuppositions that are largely modern in form. Niebuhr's work, however, does give expression to the intent of orthodoxy, which, at a minimum, has held that it is the unique place of the self in the created order that constitutes the situation, though not the explanation, of sin. And understandably, given the existentialist dimension of his concern, Niebuhr's own analysis translates the traditional intent into an element of a theology for freedom. "Anxiety," he says, quoting Søren Kierkegaard, "is the dizziness of freedom."[2]

The view of selfhood underlying Kierkegaard's (and Niebuhr's) interpretation of anxiety has already been introduced in the discussion of Sartre's view of creativity (see pp. 22–24 above), for on this matter a core of agreement may be found in Sartre, Kierkegaard, and Whitehead. All three view the self as a succession of moments of self-creation (or, as we would say, following the later Sartre and Whitehead, *contextual* self-creation). Kierkegaard writes that the self

is constantly occupied in striving, (but this) does not mean that he has . . . a goal toward which he strives, and that he would be finished when he reached this goal. No, he strives infinitely, is constantly in process of becoming. . . . As long as he is an existing individual, he is in the process of becoming.[3]

The glorious aura of potentiality that this view conveys must be balanced by its dizzying insecurity. No accomplishment of character is final, no achievement is conclusive. Each moment's potentiality reintroduces the option to renew or to reject the aims adopted in the past. Underlying each momentary decision there is no comfortingly continuous self, no abiding moral essence. Again and again the past achievement of selfhood is called into question, and one must recreate oneself anew.

Sartre observes that the self is "frightened" by this unsettledness—"there is something distressing for each of us . . . in the act of this tireless creation. . . ."[4] This judgment receives interesting confirmation in the work of Paulo Freire. Freire points out that a "fear of freedom" exists among oppressed peoples, as well as among their oppressors (though for different reasons), because freedom is a constant responsibility requiring perpetual risk. "The oppressed," he says, "are inhibited from waging the struggle for freedom so long as they feel incapable of running the risks it requires."[5]

The self shrinks from freedom, when freedom is properly understood. In spite of the fact that contextual creativity is given as the "essence" of selfhood, and thus as its potential, this essence is experienced as a dubious gift. A surer essence is longed for, one that is unencumbered by the problematic contingencies of a restricting context or one that is rid altogether of the agony of uncertain choice. The "solution" to anxiety, then, is to deny in one way or another the human nature—perched "at the juncture of nature and spirit"—that gives it rise. That is, the solution to anxiety is to deny human freedom.

The Forms of Sin: Pride

When we turn from sin's situation to consider the forms of sin, we find widespread in traditional theology a twofold classification. This dual structure is already implicit in the myth of the fall. One form of sin, reflected in Adam and Eve's rejection of the limits inherent in their natural situation (Gen. 3:1–7), has usually been called *pride*. The other, evident in Adam's blaming Eve and Eve's blaming the serpent (3:8–13), has been called *sensuality*. Pride is the denial of the limits appropriate to being human, the effort to be, like God, without restrictions. Sensuality is the denial of the powers appropriate to being human, the effort to be, like the animals, without responsibility. We shall examine each.[6]

Once again it is Reinhold Niebuhr, more than anyone else in modern theology, who has conveyed the subtlety and power of traditional Christian reflection on the nature of sin.[7] About pride Niebuhr writes:

The real evil in the human situation, according to the prophetic interpretation, lies in man's unwillingness to recognize and acknowledge the weakness, finiteness and dependence of his position, in his inclination to grasp after a power and security which transcend the possibilities of human existence, and in his effort to pretend a virtue and knowledge which are beyond the limits of mere creatures. The whole burden of the prophetic message is that there is only one God . . . and that the sin of man consists in the vanity and pride by which he imagines himself, his nations, his cultures, his civilizations to be divine. Sin is thus the unwillingness of man to acknowledge his creatureliness and dependence upon God and his effort to make his own life independent and secure. It is the "vain imagination" by which man hides the conditioned, contingent and dependent character of his existence and seeks to give it the appearance of unconditioned reality.[8]

The pride condemned in Christian theology is not a wholesome self-appreciation; it is, as Niebuhr says, the self's denial of its "dependent character." Pre-eminently, pride is the denial of our dependence upon God. Hence St. Paul is speaking of pride when he says that sin is "whatever does not proceed from faith," where faith means "constantly living out of the 'grace' of God."[9] The same point is made evident in Jesus' parable of the rich fool who imagines himself secure, independent, by reason of his grain-filled barns (Luke 12:19–20).

Yet the denial of our dependencies upon other persons—actually, our interdependencies—also comes in for strict biblical denunciation. The denial of dependency always involves the denial of the full worth of that to which one is related. The man who "think[s] of himself more highly than he ought to think" (Rom. 12:3) inevitably minimizes the other to whom he is indebted (cf. Rom. 12:3–8). The consequence of this is injustice and exploitation. The Bible's specific, uncompromising condemnation of injustice is absolutely clear (see, e.g., Deut. 24:14–15; Isa. 58:6–7, 61:1–4, 8; Jer. 22:13–17; Matt. 25:31–46; Luke 4:16–30). And even though the exploitation of persons is the primary concern, at one point God's wrath is proclaimed against Egypt because it ignores its debt to the Nile (Ezek. 29:3). Pride is never pure, but in whatever guise it appears, its inner logic drives toward the denial of all dependency. Increasingly, that which is finite and dependent is imagined to be that which is not, that which is "mortal" is mistaken for "immortality" (Rom. 1:23).

In a theology for freedom, where freedom is viewed as contextual creativity, pride is the denial of freedom's contextual side. It is the failure to acknowledge that we live from an environment of material and spiritual resources and restrictions that are not our own.

The denial of contextuality can take several forms, one of which is ingratitude. Ingratitude is a forgetfulness of the sustenance of that on which we depend. The failure to acknowledge the sustenance of God's loving-kindness is the main concern of the prophetic voice in Scripture.

The passage noted above from Ezekiel (29:3), however, reminds us that all ingratitude is condemned, not simply ingratitude to God. For all ingratitude stems from a lie, from a disregard of the sheer givenness of those resources that sustain and enrich our freedom. Ingratitude is indifference to grace.

Ingratitude appears to be a less "deadly" form of pride than are arrogance and injustice, about which we shall speak next, because ingratitude seems to involve no immediate hurt to others. But one wonders whether ingratitude is not in some respects more basic; perhaps it lies at the root of the arrogant violation of the limits of freedom and the injustice to which this leads. Insensitive to the ways that nature sustains us, for example, we presume to use it at will, upsetting thereby the tenuous ecology of physical existence. A similar dynamic occurs in what we may call the spiritual ecology. We become insensitive to the gifts others bestow upon us by their very presence, and thus we tear the fragile web of the human community. And we hide from ourselves the sustenance of divine grace, mysteriously incarnate in daily, simple things. Blinded to that all-encompassing community in which "we live and move and have our being" (Acts 17:23), we think that we sustain ourselves, attributing to ourselves an importance belied by reality. But with skillful deception (to be considered below), ingratitude, and so the other prides it may foster, does not acknowledge what it knows. It ignores the sustenance of the context of our lives. Ultimately, like all sin, ingratitude is untruth.

A second form of pride is arrogance, the denial of the limits inherent in freedom's context. The story in Genesis 3 is interesting in this regard, not only because the sin it highlights is pride in the form of arrogance, but also because of its handling of the limitation at issue and the consequences of violating it. Nothing in the story suggests that the restriction is arbitrarily imposed, commanded by God simply in order to obtain obedience; it is treated as a limit inherent in paradisial existence as such. That is why the logic moves, not from disobedience to divine wrath to punishment, but from disobedience directly to the punishment it entails. "You shall not eat . . . lest you die" (3:3) and "When you eat . . . you will be like God" (3:5)—which display a curious consistency in the fact that becoming "like God" signals the "death" of Adam and Eve's intended humanity—are both depicted as the inevitable consequence of a violation of the limits inherent in the human situation. The denial of limits is destructive, not because an offended God destroys the disobedient, but because it falsifies the human capabilities inherent in the creation that God brings into being.

If, in terms of the text, this interpretation of the myth might be open to question, the insight it contains seems fully warranted in other ways. The analysis offered in Chapter Two sought to show that "unlimited freedom" is, in the strict sense, a self-contradictory notion. No freedom is unlimited; no freedom is absolute. There are restrictions inherent to freedom itself, one of them being that creative freedom requires a context. Each such context, moreover, makes some things possible and other things impossible. The combination of creativity's essential needs, and the contingent character of its specific context, gives rise to that set of limits appropriate to the manifold possibilities for freedom's realization in that situation. These are the limits intrinsic to freedom. These are the limits urged by the God of freedom. But to this arrogance is oblivious. Savoring the illusion of limitlessness, arrogance violates freedom's boundaries. In so doing it sins against freedom and against the God of freedom.

One of the limits intrinsic to the nature of freedom is freedom's equity. No self merits more than another the richness of resource whereby its capacity for self-creativity may be enhanced and preserved. The denial of freedom's equity is injustice. Injustice, thus, is a form of arrogance.

The God who chooses freedom chooses, too, that equity inherent in freedom. Christian faith therefore insists upon the universality of divine love, the free God's impartial love of each moment of freedom. And the God who seeks freedom's increase confronts the creatures with the demand that each of us cherish the freedom of the other as we cherish our own. For Christian faith, political and social justice and injustice are religious categories. Doing injustice is sin; doing justice is obedience. Indeed, if worship means "to obey" or "to serve," then to worship the God of freedom means, fundamentally, to seek the protection of freedom, the nurture of freedom, and freedom's increase. The equation of worship and doing justice appears throughout the Scriptures. Isaiah 58:6–7 is an example.

> Is not this the fast that I choose:
>   to loose the bonds of wickedness,
>   to undo the thongs of the yoke,
>   to let the oppressed go free,
>   and to break every yoke?
> Is it not to share your bread with the hungry,
>   and bring the homeless poor into your house;
>   when you see the naked, to cover him,
>   and not to hide yourself from your own flesh?

A similar understanding is evident in Romans 12 where Paul, discussing the demands of "spiritual worship," describes an egalitarian community in which mutual sustenance nourishes the development of individual diversity. The biblical mind knows that what *we* call the "spiritual" dimensions of freedom cannot be divorced from what *we* call its "material" rootage. It is not tempted by the fiction that freedom is disincarnate, unrelated to physical, psychological, sociological, and political conditions. Hence in its portrayal of one's service to God it includes the elements of justice—showing hospitality, feeding the hungry, liberating the oppressed, freeing the captive, paying the laborer a just wage, etc.—and insists that its absence, injustice, is sin.

For Christian theology, the perpetuation of any freedom unfulfilled—the impoverished freedom of the Latin American peasant, the oppressed freedom of the black South African, the powerless freedom of the American minorities, the shallow freedom of the bored middle class, the arrogant freedom of the oppressor, the malnourished freedom of masses almost everywhere—the perpetuation of any inequity, is sin, the sin of pride. And acquiescence to this perpetuation is another form of sin, the sin of sensuality, to which we now turn our attention.

The Forms of Sin: Sensuality

Sensuality is the second major category of sin in traditional Christian thinking. The term "sensuality" is somewhat misleading (though not altogether so, as we shall see). The fundamental Christian stricture is not against the sensual or the sexual, as such, even in its present "fallen" condition. This is not fully clear in part because of the powerful influx into Christian discourse, almost from its start, of a bias against the material body and its functions, which we may loosely designate as "platonic." This influence, however, can be exaggerated.

From the second-century Apologists, in whose works a clear theological anthropology began to take shape, through Augustine, who set the tone, at least, of orthodoxy, the equation of sexuality and sin was pretty consistently avoided. Even when theologians, after Tertullian in the third century, began to hold that our inherited corruption or sinfulness, our solidarity with Adam, is somehow transmitted in the act of physical generation, they were reasonably careful to view intercourse as the vehicle of sin's transmission, not as itself sinful.[10] Still, what we have called the platonic bias has taken its toll, if for no other reason than that popular expressions of orthodoxy, particularly on this subject, have not bothered to decipher the subtle—and sometimes obscure and inconsistent—qualifications of orthodoxy's fathers. At least in this area of piety, the Christian "old" testament, unwittingly, has probably been the Platonic dialogues as much as the Hebrew Bible, whose full appreciation of the physical dimension of our lives is altogether apparent.

Sensuality, we said earlier, is the self's denial of its unique powers, its claim to be, like the animals, without responsibility. In Niebuhr's words, it is "the self's undue identification with and devotion to particular desires and impulses within itself."[11] Christian theology has generally maintained that human agency is not reducible to the forces that act upon us, whether these forces be external or internal. Thus Adam's attempt to explain his action solely in terms of Eve's action, and Eve's effort to reduce her action to the serpent's "beguilement"—both are refusals to own up to the margin of agency that the human self enjoys over and above the power of the forces that influence it, and thus both are denials of the distinct responsibility that the self has for itself. Sensuality, then, is the pretense that we are nothing more than, that we are reducible to, that we are puppets of, the forces that form the context of our lives.[12]

The frequent biblical injunctions against various expressions of the sin of sensuality may be seen, fundamentally, as pleas to preserve in practice the distinction between human beings and the animals. The "works of the flesh" listed by Paul in Galatians 5:19–20, for example, have no special relationship to the body or to sex. Most of them are quite *un*related to the physical body, e.g., idolatry, sorcery, enmity, strife, jealousy, anger, selfishness, dissention, party spirit, envy. Yet they are sins of sensuality; in them the self succumbs to the dominance of internal and external forces, refusing to acknowledge its responsibility for itself. Animals, presumably, do not distance themselves from their desires; anything like what we may call the ego or self of the animal seems to be simply identical with the organism's dominant drives at a given time. The sin of sensuality involves the pretense that the human self, like that of the animal, is identical to the passions, drives, and other forces that impinge upon it, and thus the attempt to evade responsibility for the disposition of these influences—psychological, social, political, etc.[13]

For a theology which understands freedom to be contextual creativity, sensuality is the denial of freedom's creative dimension. Sensuality is freedom's refusal to acknowledge its transcendence over context; it is the emptying of creativity into the contextual labyrinth.

In personal forms of sensuality, freedom retreats from its own power, its own agency, claiming to be bound to the dictates of bodily urges, astronomical signs, peer pressure, social precedent, the dictates of the Spirit, the necessities of good business, destiny, bad genes, its own past, etc. The self does not use the senses and the passions, for example, for enrichment and variation in a careful artistry of becoming; it becomes its passions. In the long run, usually, the result is a person for whom passion is exhausted and the life of the senses monotonous. The self does not treat compromise, departures from the ideal, as one possibility among others, for the choice of which it is responsible; the self becomes the captive of compromise. The consequence is an "individual" who is only an element within a system, a cog in the machine of corporate morality. Creativity is virtually extinguished, a mere abstraction.

In social forms of sensuality, the world is accepted as it is. The self loses its vision; the present stability is baptized; a new future is feared. Rationalizing the present, logic is domesticated.[14] The self, guilty of sensuality, resigns itself to poverty (usually that of others), sighing, "You will always have the poor with you" (Mark 14:7), curiously unwilling to conclude with similar logic that we must acquiesce to sin because the New Testament teaches the persistence of sin in the world. Or it murmurs, "You will (always) hear of wars and rumors of wars" (Matt. 24:6), assuming, apparently, that mere rumors are no improvement over the real thing. Sensuality is uncritical in its reading of tradition and of the present age. It ignores alternatives. It accepts the given, losing a feel for the difference between "what is" and "what might be."

Precisely stated, the "sin" of sensuality lies not in the fact that the self accepts the given world, but that the given it accepts has been falsified, stripped of potentiality. Sensuality excludes creativity because creativity invokes the possible. The problem is that the creative task is frequently doomed to failure. In various ways context forms hard, often tragic, boundaries which creativity cannot trespass. At any given time, many possibilities are only abstract possibilities, incapable of present realization. One of the sources of anxiety, Niebuhr has noted, is our inability to locate these boundaries with much precision. We are dizzied by the contradiction between the panorama of possibility that we see clearly and the restrictive limits that elude advance measurement. We test the ideal and fail. The task is tiring. In order to escape it we renounce it by renouncing possibility altogether, and thus creativity as well. We succumb to the falsified given. What is must be, what might be is forgotten—this is sensuality.

In a formal sense, pride and sensuality are equally betrayals of human nature. Each denies something that is essential to selfhood and integral to the divine purpose for the world. The Christian consensus throughout history, however, has been that the more fundamental sin is pride.[15] The reasons for this traditional judgment are more historical than theological in character. The affirmation of human freedom, especially as it pertains to the exercise of creativity, was weak indeed before the nineteenth century, as we indicated in Chapter One (even though, as we are trying to show, that affirmation is rooted firmly in the heart of Christian faith). Hence there was little reason to regard sensuality, which is the denial of creativity, with any particular suspicion, *except* where sensuality was viewed reductively as sexual license.[16] In addition, there is the simple fact that, now as always, the active bombast of pride gains greater notice than does the passive cowering of sensuality. Finally, those who control a given society will find the pride of their subjects more difficult to deal with than their acquiescence, so that concern about pride will always have "official" sanction. For these reasons it has been natural to make more of the sin of pride—its abuse of power, its moral and intellectual pretensions, etc.— than the quieter sin of sensuality.

The situation in the technological West may call for a reversal of theological concern, though, again, for purely historical reasons. Herbert Marcuse and others have pointed out the skill with which modern technological society manipulates private space and time no less than the public sphere.[17] Put simply, social efficiency depends upon economic productivity which in turn depends upon consumption; satisfactory rates of consumption, however, require the creation of needs to consume— "false needs," Marcuse calls them—through advertising, the programming of cultural models, economic incentives, etc. Few people today would deny that this "artificial" imposition of needs has a profound impact upon individual and social value structures. But the deeper problem lies in the fact that the forces of manipulation are so endearing, so pleasing. Throughout history, pleasure has usually been attainable through the exercise of creativity beyond established structures. The peasant and the slave, for example, found joy primarily in their small margin of transcendence over the oppressive system. The pleasure of the spiritual, the story, the game, etc., no less than the space in which these were celebrated, were products of creativity. Today, the "joys" most of us in technological societies thrive upon are integral to the system and given by the system. The tendency, then, is to abandon creativity and to sink into the automated serenities of the established order. The path of sensuality is tempting not only because it, like pride, allows us to escape the dizzy anxiety of freedom, but also because it, unlike pride, inundates us in a reliable rush of pleasures. Heedless of St. Paul's injunction (Rom. 12:2), we are thoroughly "conformed to this world," for never since Eden have the "principalities and powers" of this world been so beguiling.

The Strategy of Sin: Self-Deception

We have not exhausted the Christian understanding of the forms of sin even though what we lack is not some third type of sin. Yet to be considered is self-deception, which is not another type of sin so much as it is a compounding of the two forms of sin already discussed. Self-deception is that enveloping strategy whereby the sin of the self is hidden from the self by the self.

The note of deception appears in the Genesis account of the fall where Eve says, "The serpent beguiled me, and I ate" (3:13). In the New Testament, deceit, cunning, trickery, and lies are frequently associated with sin, as Peter Hodgson has shown.[18] "The serpent," Paul says, "deceived Eve by his cunning" (2 Cor. 11:3), and he acknowledges, "sin . . . deceived me and . . . killed me" (Rom. 7:11). But the entire New Testament knows, and presupposes, what James 1:14 makes explicit: ". . . each person is lured and enticed by his own desire." As Hodgson nicely puts it, "deception deceives itself."[19] Paul's discussion in Romans 1 is perhaps the most subtle brief analysis of this:

> For the wrath of God is revealed from heaven against all ungodliness and wickedness of men who by their wickedness suppress the truth. For what can be known about God is plain to them, because God has shown it to them. . . . So they are without excuse, for although they knew God they did not honor him as God or give thanks to him, but they became futile in their thinking and their senseless minds were darkened. Claiming to be wise, they became fools, and exchanged the glory of the immortal God for images resembling mortal man . . . (1:18–23):

The primal element of sin no less than its culminating quality is here seen to be its self-deception—"they suppress the truth." The self that does not honor God (here Paul is speaking of pride) not only acts dishonorably but also ceases to be aware of its dishonor. The sinful self's estimate of its inner dynamics, thus, cannot be trusted, for it is "futile in (its) thinking." It is deceived about its own sin. But it is *self*-deceived, because, as Paul has just said, it "knew God." It knows God, nevertheless it hides from itself its knowledge of God, and thus too it hides from itself an awareness of its own ungodliness. That is why Paul, in 1 Corinthians 4:16, refuses to count himself "acquitted" even though he is "not aware of anything against [himself]." The neat moralisms whereby we are easily condemned and easily excused are superficial. Only God will be able to "bring to light the things now hidden in darkness and . . . disclose the purposes of the heart." Sin deceives itself about its sin *and* about its self-deception.

In a theology for freedom, pride and sensuality are deceptive in a threefold sense. The prideful self is deceived in thinking that it is not contextual, and it is deceived in supposing that the pure creativity it pretends to be is even a possibility.[20] The sensual self is wrong in thinking that it is devoid of creativity, and it is deceived in thinking that a totally dependent self is possible.[21] Furthermore, these deceits of the sinful self are themselves deceptive, for although the self appears not to know the truth, in fact it does. That, at least, is the claim upon which faith insists. We know that we are free; yet, renouncing our freedom for pride or sensuality, we tell ourselves a lie about our own natures, and we believe that lie, knowing all the while, nevertheless, that we have told it to ourselves.

Were there no parallels to self-deception outside the experience of faith, the claim of faith in this regard might be less bothersome, less worthy of consideration than in fact it seems to be. But the abundance of "secular" testimonies to the phenomenon of self-deception makes faith's insistent claim difficult to dismiss. One such testimony is Sartre's oft-cited example of the young woman who intentionally suppresses her knowledge of her suitor's "baser" designs. She wishes to be desired for other than narrowly erotic reasons. Hence she consciously becomes unconscious of his erotic designs, so as to make his attention more consistent with her needs. He takes her arm—she "knows" it to be a subtle prelude to more overt advances, but at the conscious level it is divested of such meanings. She knows yet she does not know, and it is she who hides the truth from herself.[22]

Self-deception is even more elusive when its object is one's own flight from freedom. This is also witnessed to in secular literature, as Robert Penn Warren's novel *All the King's Men* illustrates. Near the close of the book the hero, Jack Burden, says:

> This has been the story of . . . a man who lived in the world and to him the world looked one way for a long time and then it looked another and very different way. The change did not happen all at once. Many things hap-

pened, and that man did not know when he had any responsibility for them and when he did not. There was, in fact, a time when he came to believe that nobody had any responsibility for anything and there was no god but the Great Twitch. At first that thought was horrible to him . . . for it seemed to rob him of a memory by which, unconsciously, he had lived. . . . But later, much later, he woke up one morning to discover that he did not believe in the Great Twitch any more. He did not believe in it because he had seen too many people live and die. He had seen [some] . . . live and the ways of their living had nothing to do with the Great Twitch. . . . He had seen his two friends . . . live and die. Each had killed the other. Each had been the doom of the other. . . . But at the same time . . . his friends had been doomed . . . they had nothing to do with any doom under the godhead of the Great Twitch. They were doomed, but they lived in the agony of will. . . . "History is blind, but man is not."[23]

Warren's "memory" (that which we know) by which we live unconsciously (that which we do not know) expresses well the "knowing but not knowing" which Christian faith calls self-deception. It preserves in nontheological terms the essential claim of Christian doctrine, namely, that the sinful self is responsible for its sin, is responsible for the suppression of its knowledge of its sin, is responsible for its denial of that responsibility, and knows it. The "memory" by which we live is too relentless, and too persistently confirmed by the ways of our lives, to let us believe *completely* in the godheads of the Great Twitch or the Great Potentate. We are neither pure reflex nor pure monarch, and even if we think we are, there is a "memory" within us that knows better.

The Objectification of Sin: Original Sin

Self-deception is not a type or a form of sin; it is the capacity of sin in either of its forms to "subjectify" itself, to hide itself in itself. In a similar way, what has been called original sin in Christian theology is a capacity of sin, not a type. It is sin's ability to "objectify" itself, that is, to manifest itself beyond itself so that sin somehow takes on a separate structure or status, assuming a power of its own.

In terms of its dramatic content, the doctrine of original sin proclaims that the sin which resulted in Adam and Eve's "fall and expulsion from paradise is transmitted from generation to generation, so that all [their] descendants . . . must be regarded as being of a 'perverted' or 'depraved' nature."[24] In Christian history the doctrine is no doubt grounded in Paul who held that "in Adam all die" (1 Cor. 15:22; cf. Rom. 5:15, 19). The crucial Pauline statement of this is Romans 5:12: "Therefore . . . sin came into the world through one man and death through sin, and so death spread to all men because [or "inasmuch as"] all men sinned." The result, in Paul's view, is that sin takes on the form of an enslaving power (Rom. 5:21; 6:6, 17, 20; 7:17, 20) that dominates the "present evil age" (Gal. 1:4) wherein rule malign "principalities" and "powers" (Rom. 8:38; Eph. 3:10, 6:12, Col. 2:15) and "elemental spirits" (Gal. 4:3, 9; Col. 2:20).

Early postbiblical theological statements vary considerably on the nature and extent of sin's objectification, and on the manner of its transmission.[25] The notion that the circumstance of our lives, the world in which we live, has been profoundly corrupted since Adam is commonly shared —"corruption gathered force against men," Athanasius said. In Tertullian, of the third century, the judgment became standard that we and not only our world are affected, that the self since Adam has some inescapable (though not essential) bias toward sin. But not until the fourth century, and first clearly in Augustine, was it held that because of Adam all are guilty. The means whereby original sin, however it was understood, was said to have been transmitted did not receive much clarity before the time of Tertullian, who taught that Adam's infection is passed on in physical generation. However, the dominant view then, and probably until early in the fifth century, was a vague notion of our mystical oneness with Adam, and thus our own "directly" rather than "indirectly" transmitted involvement in Adam's sin. The standard text for this was the mistaken, but common, translation of Romans 5:12: ". . . sin came into the world through one man . . . *in whom* [rather than the correct 'because' or 'inasmuch as'] all men sinned" (italics added). Augustine, too, followed the "in whom" rendering of this passage, but for him its meaning was determined by this doctrine of the physical transmission of sin, which Augustine urged more strongly than did any of his predecessors. Augustine tempered the doctrine on occasion, as for example when he appended to Paul's statement, "all have sinned" (Rom. 3:23), his own qualification, "whether in Adam or in themselves."[26] But it was not to be compromised. Eventually, the doctrine that through physical generation we inherit from Adam a corrupt world, a personal nature prone to sin, and the guilt of the fall became orthodoxy.

It is not uncommon to dismiss the view of original sin derived from Augustine as being excessive if not absurd. Given the resources of the fourth-century worldview, however, it would be difficult to conceive of a more "empirical" or a clearer way of affirming the objective givenness that pride and sensuality take on in the historical process, or the power of these objective structures over our lives, or our inability to reliably distinguish their actions upon us and our willful complicity with them. But Augustine's way of explaining this givenness, its power, and its elusiveness, is no more the point at issue than are the mythological categories utilized by St. Paul. The important claim is that sin is objectified.

The objective structures which sin assumes may usefully be divided into three categories—personal, social, and natural. It is the personal structure with which we are, in a sense, most intimately acquainted. Moreover, traditional Christian reflection has been most intent to clarify this personal dimension. Hence we shall take it as our starting point.

The *personal objectification of sin,* i.e., the objectification of the self's sin into the structure of the self, comes to light in an examination of our own experience of the "divided will" or the "divided self," as it has been called. The classic text for this is Romans 7:14–25, in which Paul identifies the conflict between what the self *wills* and what the self *does:* "I can will what is right, but I cannot do it. For I do not do the good I want, but the evil I do not want I do" (vv. 18b–19). Paul's explanation of this is that sin is a power that has come to dwell within the self: "Now if I do what I do not want, it is no longer I that do it, but sin which dwells within me" (v. 20).

Still, the war is between two "parts" of the self, not between the self and some foreign intruder (except insofar as the self's sin is an intruder upon the self's true or essential nature). For, just as Paul aligns the "law of God" with his "inmost self" (v. 7:22), so also he associates the "law of sin" with the other dimension of the self which he calls "my members" (v. 23) or "my flesh" (v. 24), i.e., the "I" which is "carnal" (v. 14). These terms do not refer to something "in" the self; they refer to a particular stance which the self takes, namely, that attitude of mind which is "hostil[ity] to God" (8:7). In short, although the self experiences itself as if it were the captive of some alien force residing within, that force is in fact an element of the self. The conflict is the self's conflict with itself, a war between the "I" that "can will" and the same "I" that "cannot do."[27]

St. Augustine clarifies this inner struggle in a passage from his *Confessions:*

> For this was what I was longing to do; but as yet I was bound by the iron chain of my own will. . . . I was rather an unwilling sufferer than a willing actor. And yet it was through me that habit had become an armed enemy against me, because I had willingly come to be what I unwillingly found myself to be. . . . Thus with the baggage of the world I was sweetly burdened, as one in slumber, and my musings on thee were like the efforts of those who desire to awake, but who are still overpowered with drowsiness and fall back into deep slumber. . . . [A] man will usually defer shaking off his drowsiness when there is a heavy lethargy in his limbs; and he is glad to sleep on even when his reason disapproves. . . . [T]he law of sin is the tyranny of habit, by which the mind is drawn and held, even against its will. Yet it deserves to be so held because it willingly falls into the habit.[28]

Augustine's reference to sleep and habit is instructive, for it indicates that the structure we are considering is not altogether unique. The self that cannot do what it wills to do makes itself known to us in trivial things ("I know I should lose five pounds, but . . .") as well as grave ones. And the reference to habit is especially enlightening if we understand that habit may be a falsification.

Habit insofar as it is morally relevant is the pretension that what we shall call an "endorsed preference" is an "enforced preference." The self, freedom, is creativity *and* context. Context is not simply the external environment of the self; it becomes ingredient in the self. In this way, context enforces certain of its preferences upon the present moment of becoming, because alternatives to these preferences are genuinely impossible. Other preferences, however, come accompanied by their alternatives. They are influences, not compulsions, which are actualized only by virtue of the endorsement of the newly becoming moment. Habit is a function of the self whereby certain of its own preferences are ratified in advance, we might say, so that they are treated as necessities. Thus, habit is a falsification because what the self treats as necessities, enforced preferences, are in fact subjects of its own endorsement. Clearly, habit is in most cases a valuable falsification because it allows the self to dispense with some evaluations in order to concentrate on others. But habitual preferences, like nonhabitual ones, may also be destructive. Even so, they linger on as a force within the self. Habit is a *given,* derived by the present moment of experience from its predecessors. Thus Augustine's image of drowsiness is appropriate, connoting our weakness before an "outside" force that enters in and grips us. But it is *our* given, something we impose upon ourselves. We have not been chained; we slumber.

The inner struggle between the self that knows and the same self that lingers in habitual drowsiness is all too real to us. We know of the consumeristic mania that trivializes our lives; we know of the rapid depletion of nature's resources that threatens our survival; we know of multitudes who suffer brutal oppression; we know of those excessive interests of ours that deprive loved ones of needed intimacy; we know that our own socio-economic system flaunts inequities of wealth, power, and opportunity; we know of futility, malnourishment, starvation—we know, yet sleepily we continue in our destructive ways as captives of habit. Succumbing to a heavy lethargy of soul, even when our inmost self disapproves, we gladly sleep. Augustine quotes St. Paul's expression of the resultant agony: "Wretched man that I am! Who will deliver me . . . ?" (Rom. 7:24).

The *social objectifications of sin* are those embedded in structures expressive of patterned interpersonal relationships, viz., the structures of relations between economic and social classes, sexes, ages, and races. Nothing is said in the New Testament about the power of these social realities. One obvious reason is that the first-century worldview lacked the combination of consciousness and theory to make them explicit. It knew about masters and slaves, to be sure, but it knew nothing about the psychological, sociological, and economic structures which arise from and perpetuate the master/slave relationship in some independence of the decisions of particular masters and slaves. Furthermore, whatever intuitive knowledge of these realities they might have possessed, the early Christians' expectation of the imminent end of this age made such matters unimportant. In later generations, "when the end was postponed indefinitely, the demand that 'everyone should remain in the state in which he was called' (1 Cor. 7:20) readily became the banner of social conservatism."[29] If such a use of Paul's words was illicit, it was nonetheless effective in promoting a disinterest in the nature of social structures, to say nothing of changing them.

Even though the Bible is silent about the character of social structures, as we understand them, it is pervaded by a sense of the corporate dimension of individual life. This is abundantly clear in the Old Testament, but it is also apparent in Paul's consistent association of individual sinfulness with the corrupted state of the world. Paul's primary category for referring to this condition was the "principalities and powers" which we have already mentioned. This sphere of cosmic powers, according to Paul, is not essentially perverse; it belongs to the world as it was created by God (Rom. 8:38).[30] Nevertheless, it is now corrupt, and it now encompasses us, holding us tightly in its grasp. As Bultmann says, it "gains the upper hand over the individual," so that it comes "to constitute an independent super-self over all individual selves."[31] Finally, although it controls us, it "does not come over man . . . as a sheer curse of fate, but grows up out of [man] himself."[32]

In exploring a theology for freedom, we cannot help being struck by the parallels between Paul's "principalities and powers" and the social and political structures within which we live. We have only recently begun to investigate these structures. Even yet we know little about their internal dynamics (as is indicated by the trial-and-error character of economics and sociology) and not much more about the mode of their power over us (as the diversity in social psychology reveals). We do know, however, that structures of race, money, sex, etc., have a firm power over our lives only tenuously related to our planning and action, in spite of the fact that these structures exist only because we do live and plan and act. But once activated by us, they control us tenaciously, determining the poverty or richness of the environment of our creative freedom.

Although they can never guarantee the maturation of freedom, these social structures favor the freedom of some persons to astonishing degrees. Others they deprive. Mechanisms of racism, sexism, and class, deeply ingrained in dominant forms of cultural expression, insinuate themselves into individuals, their language, their actions, and their understandings of what is possible. The mechanisms, and the social patterns which give rise to them, reinforce one another in an antiphonal dirge of exploitation and injustice. Consequently, an overwhelming burden of misery falls upon the victims. But *all* are warped in mind and spirit— baptizing things as they are, feeling that they somehow deserve their fortune or misfortune, unable to dream of a better world, and unaware that they are warped.

When the sin of injustice is viewed as the denial of freedom's equity, few people would deny that injustice is structured into the fabric of our lives. This may be seen in the economic sphere, even from the standpoint of middle-class Americans.[33] They are by no means oblivious to the disproportion in incomes among working groups that is dictated by our economic system. To illustrate with the most glaring example, the median net earnings of all medical doctors (from their professional practice alone) was $72,500 in 1974.[34] This was more than five times the median income of all U.S. families (including those with more than one member employed), and it was almost five times the income of those groups whose education is comparable to that of physicians.[35] But the middle class is not the most disadvantaged. When we recall that 20 percent of the U.S. population receives one-half the personal income, we realize that an even more shameful disparity exists between the highest paid identifiable working groups and a large proportion of the 80 percent who must share the other one-half of the personal income. The income ratio for physicians and farm laborers, for example, is over twenty to one.[36]

These, however, are certainly not the most disturbing facts one could cite, for the gross inequities within the United States pale considerably in the light of worldwide disparities. The per capita income of Americans in 1972 ($5,056) was almost twenty-three times that of persons living in the developing countries ($220).[37] The trend is toward a greater disparity—at the beginning of the nineteenth century the difference in per capita income between poor and rich countries was about 1:2; today the ratio in real, not merely nominal, terms is about 1:20.[38] And this real difference results in real, not merely statistical, suffering and deprivation—the infant mortality rate in developing countries is ten times higher than that in developed countries, with one-half of those deaths being related to inadequate diet; 210 million children in the world today are threatened by permanent brain damage because they suffer from malnutrition; one-half billion persons are starving; and another one-half to one and one-half billion have a seriously insufficient protein intake; one-third to one-half of the world's population lives without access to any type of medical care. Such unrelieved deprivation inexorably moves its victims toward that final human sacrifice, the loss of hope:

> Sometimes I think, "If I die, I won't have to see my children suffering as they are." Sometimes I even think of killing myself. So often I see them crying, hungry; and there I am, without a cent to buy them some bread. I think, "My God, I can't face it! I'll end my life. I don't want to look anymore."[39]

In the world of these realities, freedom is nearly a fiction. The question, then, is not whether we live amid unjust structures; it is whether their grasp can be broken. The answer, probably, is no, not without radical changes that those of us in privileged positions do not care to take seriously. We prefer to find solutions that would reform the present principalities and powers. The evidence is pretty strong, however, that these structures evade our reformist remedies.

One sign of the incorrigible nature of our present economic structures is the failure of that solution not long ago proposed as a perfectly rational and moderate cure for global inequities in wealth. Without destroying the existing systems in rich nations, it was said, the creation of multinational corporations (MNCs) would enable the development of poor nations by introducing financial capital into these nations, expanding their business sector, creating jobs, and increasing personal incomes. Thorough studies show that the opposite occurs on almost every count.[40] In Latin America from 1957 to 1965, only 17 percent of MNC investment funds was imported; the balance was derived from local sources in the poorer nations. Of this locally derived 83 percent, almost one-half (46 percent) was then used to buy out existing locally controlled firms whose profits would have been retained domestically. The net profits of the MNCs, however, were "repatriated" on an average of 79 percent. The resultant drying up of funds in these nations, in addition to the trend toward modernized production methods, actually increased unemployment, so that the figure now exceeds 30 percent of the active work force. The gap between the rich and poor classes widens. To illustrate, during the 1960s in Brazil, where the MNCs are strong, the income of the top 5 percent increased from 27.8 percent to 36.8 percent of the national income, while that of the lowest 40 percent dropped from 10.6 percent to 8.1 percent. Between the rich and poor nations the gap also widens. As Ronald Müller concludes, "in aggregate terms the poor countries of the world are now ironically helping to finance the rich countries, i.e., the financial outflows from [less developed countries] far exceed the inflows."[41]

Were any of us, as visitors from another planet, to observe the consequences of our national and global economic systems, we would conclude without hesitation that it ought to be changed, immediately and fundamentally. From within, however, we know how thoroughly the system controls us. The straps of power are drawn tightly. In the United States, 60 percent of productive assets are controlled by 200 corporations, which are in turn owned by less than 5 percent of the population. This means that the effective economic power in this country rests in the hands of less than 100,000 people.[42] But that, though a momentous difficulty for any prospect of change, is not the deeper problem. The deeper problem, we know (if only dimly), is that the thoughts, feelings, and actions of all of us are tightly controlled by the economic principalities and powers, the very powers that we create and sustain. In a factual sense, we are the enemies of freedom, and enemies of the God of freedom. We wish that we had never settled into these comfortable structures of inhumanity, although they grew up out of our own wills, but now that we are here we do not move beyond them to new forms of social and economic organization where freedom and justice are more nearly one. St. Augustine said that we willingly enter the bondage wherein we unwillingly find ourselves. It is also true that we *willingly remain* in the bondage wherein we unwillingly find ourselves. We wish we were not here, but we choose to stay.

The *objectification of sin in nature,* the third category of sin's objectification, is evident in that impoverishment of resources and corruption of processes which result from our prideful exploitation of nature and our slothful assent to that exploitation. One cannot condemn all adaptations of nature, for some adaptations enhance nature as well as ourselves. The order of nature is not sacrosanct, but nature does have rights that are. For if, as Chapter Two maintained, nature itself possesses some modicum of freedom, then any adaptation that on balance diminishes nature's creative potential is directly, and in the strictest sense, a sin against nature. In an indirect but powerful way, the exploitation of nature is also a sin against human freedom, for the impoverishment of nature is the impoverishment of the context of our lives. Only now is science beginning to become concerned enough to seek to identify the structures of nature's exploitation. Some things, like the production of gases that irrevocably destroy essential natural processes, may be judged wholesale. Other things, such as strip mining, must to some extent be decided on a circumstantial basis. What is urgently required in most instances is more data, and great caution until it is available. The mandate for research and for caution is clear, from the standpoint of Christian faith, for technological structures of exploitation are no less objectifications of sin than are political structures of tyranny or spiritual structures of indifference. In our time, "cursed is the ground because of you" (Gen. 3:17) has a special relevance.

The Consequence of Sin: Death

Sin and death are fairly commonly associated in biblical thought—"The soul that sins shall die" (Ezek. 18:4). The nature of that relationship, however, is not always clear. In Genesis 3:3 death is identified as the consequence of sin ("You shall not eat the fruit of the tree . . . lest you die"), but the claim is not followed up. In 3:19 death is mentioned, yet not as the punishment or the consequence of sin; it is simply the terminal point of that punishment (". . . till you return to the ground") and is associated with the fact that Adam was taken from dust, not with the fact that he sinned. Even so, the rabbinic teaching in the first century was that physical mortality is the result of sin, and Paul did not challenge this view (cf. Rom. 5:12–14). But it is also true that "death," in its most crucial meaning for Paul, refers to a binding condition, not to human mortality.[43] Hence, Paul says that death is already a present reality for those in sin—"When the commandment came, sin revived and I died" (Rom. 7:9; cf. vv. 10, 11, 13); "You were dead through . . . trespasses and sins" (Eph. 2:1; cf. v. 5, and Col. 2:13). In Paul, then, as in the Fourth Gospel (e.g., 5:24ff., 6:50, 8:24), the death consequent upon sin is fundamentally the condition of alienation, separation from God the giver of life. It is, therefore, in *this* death, alienation, that physical death, too, becomes the enemy (1 Cor. 15:26).

Although Paul speaks of death as the punishment for sin (Rom. 6:23; 1 Cor. 15:56), this "juristic" conception, as Bultmann calls it,[44] is less basic than another analysis of Paul's, an "organic" conception, viz., the idea that death is inherent in sin in the same way, for example, that a plant is inherent in a seed. This is most explicit in passages like Galatians 6:8 ("He who sows . . . will . . . reap corruption") and Romans 7:5 ("Our sinful passions . . . were at work . . . to bear fruit for death"), but it is also apparent in Romans 8:13 ("If you live according to the flesh you will die"). The point is that death, alienation, is not a punishment arbitrarily assigned to sin; death is built into sin, so to speak, as its necessary and unavoidable consequence.

The two elements of Paul's doctrine that we have identified—death as spiritual alienation, and death as the organic consequence of sin—were not retained with much clarity in the history of Christian theology. They were not lost or denied, but they were greatly overshadowed by the interest in physical death as the divinely assigned punishment for sin, for historical reasons that we need not examine. Whatever precedent these later concerns may find in biblical reflection, there can be little doubt that they are not the fundamental ones. In Paul, especially, it is clear that death is a "spiritual" condition that the sinful self brings upon itself.

Death is the consequence of sin, in a theology for freedom, because sin is the self's denial of its freedom and death is the culmination of that denial. Wherever freedom is unfulfilled death is present as reality and as threat. Death is the self's alienation from its own essence, its separation from its character as contextual creativity. As such, death is always to some degree a reality in life, for temporal existence never witnesses the perfect fullness of freedom. The reality of death in life is always a threat to life, because freedom is unitary. The physical, personal, and spiritual levels of freedom are not precisely divided, except to abstract thought; they are interrelated. The degree of richness freedom achieves at one level is threatened by freedom's poverty at another.

Death is present as reality and as threat at the physical level whenever the material requirements of a creative existence are lacking. Death is present in any prolonged deprivation—a stomach aching from hunger, a body burning with fever, a brain dulled to beauty, love, and acceptance. But those who are deprived, and those who deprive in order to control, know of the intrinsic connection between freedom at the material level and personal and spiritual freedoms. A tortured body threatens one's sense of worth in the human community and one's sense of meaning in the cosmos.

Death is present as reality and as threat at the personal level when the social and psychological resources necessary for becoming are denied. The self separated or alienated from other selves lacks the enrichment of the human community, the result of which may be psychic debilitation.

But the self dwelling in a poisoned community is also deprived, as we have seen. Vision is distorted, sensitivity dulled, ways of thinking canalized. The eventual effect of impoverishment at this level upon physical functioning is well known. One may suppose that death present here also affects the spiritual dimension. It is true that through careful discipline spiritual vitality may sometimes be preserved in spite of acute physical and personal deprivation, but permanent deprivation is scarcely to be recommended as a boon to spiritual strength. Lurking behind the too narrowly-based vision of God lies the threat of futility, the vision of nothingness.

Death is present at the spiritual level when freedom is deprived of its spiritual base. In Western culture this is most likely experienced as the sense of life's futility or, in our terms, the futility of freedom. The opposite of futility is the confidence that freedom has some basis in the nature of things, some ground of worth that is not subject to the caprice of history and the limits of time. For Christian faith this ground is God, as we discussed in the previous chapter. Freedom's meaning, ultimately (though by no means entirely), is its worth to and for the life of God. From this worth, freedom's penultimate value is enhanced and sustained. Spiritual death is the loss of this confidence in the ultimate worth of freedom. When death is real at this level, the substance of the other dimensions of life, personal and physical, is threatened.

Although the "death of the soul"—as we shall term this death that permeates the physical, personal, and spiritual levels of our lives—is not to be equated with human mortality, the two forms of death have a special connection. Physical death finalizes the degree to which the death of the soul has been victorious. From the standpoint of history, the self's failure to realize its freedom is, with the death of the body, rendered irrevocable. Thus, in the death of the soul, physical mortality, too, becomes the enemy.

It is not morbid to say that death infects the whole of human existence. So to speak is to acknowledge that everywhere the intended fulfillment of freedom that is sought by the God of freedom is in some measure being denied. Indeed, with St. Paul we may say—no, we *must* say—that "the whole creation has been groaning in travail until now" in "its bondage to decay" and death (see Rom. 8:18–25). Thus, too, is St. Paul's question one that is voiced by the whole creation: Who will deliver us from this body of death? (Rom. 7:24)

Notes

1. This and the remaining quotations in this paragraph are from Reinhold Niebuhr, *The Nature and Destiny of Man* (New York: Scribner's, 1955), Vol. 1, pp. 181–83.

2. Ibid., p. 252. The quotation is from Søren Kierkegaard, *The Concept of Dread* (Princeton: Princeton University Press, 1944), p. 55.

3. Søren Kierkegaard, *Concluding Unscientific Postscript* (Princeton: Princeton University Press, 1941), p. 84.

4. Jean-Paul Sartre, *The Transcendence of the Ego* (New York: Noonday Press, 1957), pp. 100, 99.

5. Paulo Freire, *Pedagogy of the Oppressed* (New York: Seabury Press, 1974), p. 32.

6. Today, one can use the terms "pride" and "sensuality" in their traditional, negative senses only with the greatest hesitation. The terms themselves, no less than the heritage of reflection which they represent, have been pretty widely distorted for the purposes of oppression. Perhaps in response, those who have been oppressed have transformed the terms, using them to refer to that which is wholesome and, indeed, essential to a viable, comprehensive sense of selfhood. A theology that seeks to support freedom must emphatically support the self-affirmation and the affirmation of the self's embodiedness that "pride" and "sensuality," respectively, have now come to connote in Third World, black, and, especially, feminist literature. At the same time, a theology for freedom that seeks, as does the present study, to unveil the mandate for freedom's affirmation at the very heart of the tradition might best proceed by retaining the terms of the tradition *in their original intent*—which was to extend freedom, not to condemn it. If, for this reason, we have chosen to depart from the contemporary use of "pride" and "sensuality," it should be clear that *we have also departed from their historic misuse,* seeking thereby to invoke the power of the theological tradition for the purpose of strengthening and informing the search for freedom in today's world.

7. See, esp., Niebuhr, *Nature and Destiny of Man,* Vol. 1, Ch. 6–9, to which the present discussion is greatly indebted.

8. Ibid., pp. 137f.

9. Rudolf Bultmann, *Theology of the New Testament* (New York: Scribner's, 1951), Vol. 1, p. 324. The Pauline statement is from Romans 14:23.

10. On this see J. N. D. Kelly, *Early Christian Doctrines* (New York: Harper, 1958), pp. 163–88, 344–74.

11. Niebuhr, *Nature and Destiny,* I, p. 228.

12. What we have called "sensuality" others have termed "sloth," "apathy," and "flight." These alternative designations are instructive. "Sloth" and "apathy" indicate the "laziness" ingredient in this betrayal of freedom. "Flight" suggests our responsibility for this laziness, the fact that our retreat into indecision itself presupposes a decision. Our term "sensuality" is intended to embrace both of these dimensions.

13. We may have discovered another reason (one quite unrelated to the so-called Platonic bias mentioned earlier) for the association of sensuality and sexuality in the theological tradition. In no other common human activity, perhaps, is the self so closely linked to its passions. Thus, sexuality may seem to furnish a rough analogy for what tradition has termed "sensuality." Of course, one term of an analogy whereby the dynamics of sensuality might be elucidated is not an *example* of sensuality, even if the expression of sexuality, like that of the other passions, could become sensuality in the theological sense. But sexual expression may nonetheless provide a uniquely appropriate model for understanding the structure of sensuality, because sexual expression so vividly recalls for us the possibility of reducing the self to natural forces.

14. Rubem Alves calls this the "logic of the dinosaur" in his splendid exploration of "imagination, creativity, and the rebirth of culture," *Tomorrow's Child* (New York: Harper & Row, 1972).

15. See Niebuhr, *Nature and Destiny,* I, pp. 186, 228.

16. Niebuhr observes that "the more Hellenistic . . . forms of Christianity. . . defined sin as primarily sensuality" (in ibid., p. 229; cf. p. 186, n. 1), but he also notes that in these instances sensuality was viewed as "sexual license" (p. 229). The parity of sensuality, in its deeper meaning, with pride has seldom if ever been realized in Christian theology.

17. Marcuse writes: "Over and above all particular manipulations in the interest of certain businesses, policies, lobbies, the general objective purpose is to reconcile the individual with the mode of existence which his society imposes on him. . . . Social needs must become individual needs, instinctual needs. And to the degree to which the production of this society requires mass production and mass consumption, these needs must be standardized, coordinated, and generalized. Certainly, these controls are not a conspiracy. . . . They are rather diffused throughout the society, exercised by the neighbors, the community, the peer groups, mass media, corporations, and (perhaps least) by the government" ("Aggressiveness in Advanced Industrial Society," in Donald E. Cutler, ed., *The Religious Situation* [Boston: Beacon Press, 1969], pp. 427f.).

18. Peter C. Hodgson, *New Birth of Freedom: A Theology of Bondage and Liberation* (Philadelphia: Fortress Press, 1976), p. 176, n. 18.

19. Ibid., p. 177 (italics removed).

20. In Chapter Two it was argued on Whiteheadian grounds that absolute creativity is a self-contradictory concept, and in Chapter Three it was shown that, even if coherent, it could not apply to the Christian God.

21. The claim that an actuality at even the lowest level of reality possesses some measure of creativity was presented in Chapter Two, in Whiteheadian terms. This claim applies only to ultimately real entities, that is, to those "actual entities," as Whitehead calls them, that collectively constitute composite objects such as trees and rocks. Composite objects as such are not creative, of course, even though their metaphysically ultimate "parts" are.

22. See Jean-Paul Sartre, *Existential Psychoanalysis,* trans. Hazel E. Barnes (New York: Philosophical Library, 1953), pp. 225ff. Stephen Crites provides an illuminating analysis of self-deception, in reference to Sartre and others, in "The Aesthetics of Self-Deception," *Soundings* 62 (Summer 1979): 107–129.

23. Robert Penn Warren, *All the King's Men* (New York: Bantam Books, 1959), pp. 435f.

24. Wilhelm Pauck, "Original Sin," in Vergilius Ferm, ed., *An Encyclopedia of Religion* (New York: Philosophical Library, 1945), p. 551.

25. For most of the material in this paragraph, except when noted otherwise, I am indebted to J. N. D. Kelly, *Early Christian Doctrines,* pp. 163–88, 344–74.

26. Cited in Reinhold Niebuhr, *Nature and Destiny,* I, p. 261.

27. Cf. Bultmann, *Theology of the New Testament,* I, pp. 232–46, and "Romans 7 and the Anthropology of Paul," in Schubert M. Ogden, ed., *Existence and Faith: Shorter Writings of Rudolf Bultmann* (New York: Living Age Books, 1960), pp. 147–57.

28. Augustine, *Confessions,* 8. 5., in Library of Christian Classics, Vol. 7 (Philadelphia: Westminster Press, 1955), pp. 164f.

29. Leander Keck, "The Son Who Creates Freedom," in Edward Schillebeeckx and Bas Van Iersel, eds., *Jesus Christ and Human Freedom*, Concilium 93 (New York: Herder and Herder, 1974), p. 75.

30. Bultmann, *Theology of the New Testament*, I, p. 230.

31. Ibid., pp. 256f.

32. Ibid., p. 256.

33. While a theology for freedom need not attempt to assemble a catalog of sins, it must go beyond merely saying that sin is objectified. It must also indicate, to the limits of its insight, where and in what form that objectification is at work in our midst. This is essential because a theology that intends to be Christian must be *for* and not merely about freedom. If God is partisan, as we claimed in Chapter Three, so, too, is any theology that seeks to be faithful to God's purpose in the world.

The effort here is to point out the structures of sin as they are manifest in American capitalism (a topic already broached, especially in reference to Marcuse), though one might as appropriately deal with racism or sexism. It should also be acknowledged, however, that everything previously said about pride and self-deception poses a special threat to the theologian. If, as Niebuhr warns, "religion is . . . a final battle ground between God and man's self-esteem" (*Nature and Destiny*, I, p. 200), then theology, which (in spite of the theologian's frequent disclaimer) attempts to reflect at least a few of God's own thoughts, is especially vulnerable to self-righteousness. Nevertheless, Christian theologians are compelled to speak, as we have explained, trusting that experience, discussion, and openness to the witness of faith will reveal our pretension and correct our errors, for others and, we hope, for ourselves.

34. *Statistical Abstract of the United States: 1976* (Bureau of Statistics, U.S. Department of Commerce), p. 80.

35. Ibid., pp. 379ff.

36. Ibid.

37. *Yearbook of National Accounts Statistics*, Vol. III, 1975 (United Nations), pp. 10, 12.

38. Ronald J. Sider, *Rich Christians in An Age of Hunger: A Biblical Study* (Downers Grove, Ill.: Intervarsity Press, 1977), p. 41. The remaining statistics in this paragraph are cited on pages 24, 36f., 32f., and 36, respectively, of Sider's very powerful study.

39. This is the statement of Iracema da Silva, resident of a Brazilian slum, quoted in Sider, *Rich Christians*, p. 31.

40. The material in this paragraph is drawn from Ronald Müller, "Poverty Is the Product," *Foreign Policy* 13 (Winter 1973–74): 71–103.

41. Ibid., p. 75. An elaborate presentation of additional evidence for the structural nature of injustice, as it relates to world hunger, may be found in Sider, *Rich Christians*, ch. 6.

42. These figures were cited in Frederick Herzog, "Liberation Theology Begins at Home," *Christianity and Crisis* 34 (May 13, 1974): 97.

43. Bultmann, *Theology of the New Testament*, I, pp. 246–49. Peter Hodgson represents this "fluid and unsystematic" Pauline distinction with the terms *thnetos* (physical mortality) and *thanatōs* (death conceived as a binding power), in *New Birth of Freedom*, p. 191.

44. Bultmann, *Theology of the New Testament*, I. p. 249.

Chapter Five

The Confirmation of Freedom:
An Understanding of Christ

The previous two chapters have a dual structure. They present basic elements of the historic Christian conceptions of God and sin, respectively; then they show how these elements of traditional thought can be transposed into an explicit theology for freedom. However interesting or even compelling the transposition of these chapters might seem to be, it remains, from the standpoint of Christian faith, what Søren Kierkegaard called a "thought-project," an experimental association of ideas. Faith and freedom *may be* associated, but we have yet to see how one could say that they *ought to be* related as we have suggested.

The ultimate warrant for a Christian affirmation of freedom's worth must inevitably be found, if at all, in reference to Jesus Christ, in whom the faith of Christians is created and sustained. What is needed, therefore, is a credible exposition of the claim that, to use Käsemann's phrase, "Jesus means freedom." Only if the Jesus who is present to Christian faith may be viewed as the confirmation of the worth of freedom can one justifiably affirm that, for Christians, God is the lure toward freedom and sin is freedom's denial. A Christian theology for freedom presupposes a Christology of freedom.

Jesus as the Gospel of Freedom

Our theological undertaking may begin with the consensus of historical scholarship that in the New Testament witness the core of Jesus' gospel is the proclamation of the kingdom of God.[1] The concept "kingdom of God" existed in extraordinary variety in the first century, the only common meaning being a dynamic one having to do with the manifestation of God's active rule. The kingdom of God was to be characterized not "by latent authority but by the exercise of power, not by an office but a function. It was not a title but a deed."[2] As proclaimed by Jesus the kingdom was a future event, yet also a present one—on this scholars seem virtually agreed, though they do not always agree on the sense of this distinction. The reign of God was so very near, as Jesus represented it, that precisely because of its imminence its power was already breaking into the present, thus requiring the hearer to decide now regarding the salvation at hand.[3] As Mark puts it: "Jesus came into Galilee . . . saying, 'The time is fulfilled, and the kingdom of God is at hand; repent, and believe in the gospel' " (1:14–15).

In spite of the fact that it is the central feature of his message, Jesus does not define the expression "kingdom of God." Its meaning is made apparent less in what he says, as such, than in the kinds of things he says or in how he says what he says. For example, William A. Beardslee has called attention to the fact that the proverbs of Jesus (shorn of their now dulling familiarity) would have stunned the serious hearer, not so much in their content as in the construction of that content.[4] "Whoever seeks to gain his life will lose it, but whoever loses his life will preserve it" (Luke 17:33) almost certainly had the effect of dramatically shaking the listener out of customary ways of looking at things. The settled guidance of the past, conventional wisdom—that was all forcefully called into question by the proverbs. These proverbs conveyed wisdom by challenging wisdom. By force of the unexpected, they moved the hearer to the edge of a new mode of thinking and living.

The parables of Jesus furnish an even clearer apprehension of the nature of the kingdom, again, because of what they *do* to the hearer. Robert W. Funk has said, "To grasp the parable in its fullness means to see what happens when the parable occurs."[5] The "point" of the parable, in its deepest sense, is what it brings about. Thus Norman Perrin and others claim that the parables of Jesus bear the reality of the kingdom of God, of God's present and coming power.[6] And because this reality is experienced as a freeing reality, Peter Hodgson has referred to the parables as "events of freedom."[7] The connection between the parables and freedom, it should be noted, lies less in the fact that freedom is sometimes their implicit theme than in the fact that they are always potentially freeing.[8] They may agitate us out of familiar patterns of thought and action, regardless of where we find ourselves, by injecting the unexpected, the unfamiliar into the familiar. They are existentially unsettling. We find in them a meaning, a point, only to discover upon further reflection how much our interpretation has missed. We try again, attempting a fuller grasp; our effort fails. Sometimes the parable comes to us with its own protection against a settled understanding, as in the Parable of the Unjust Steward (Luke 16:1–13). Here the parable itself is followed by six different interpretive statements each of which alone could serve as a summary of the "point" of the parable. William G. Doty says these conclusions were added at later times, each in an effort to capture the parable's "real" meaning.[9] If so, this was curiously appropriate, for the clearly diverse summations in conjunction with each other are as unsettling as the parable itself.

The parables of Jesus unsettle us, not because we do not know what they mean but because they mean too much. Confronted by them, we cannot relax into accepted ways of seeing things. Again and again their words shake us from our comfortable moorings. We begin to realize that their purpose is less in what they tell us than in what they do to us. Their persistent opaqueness keeps us open, wondering, exploring. In this way the parables free us, and often it is a painful freedom.

We have indicated how the message of Jesus in the New Testament may be said to constitute a gospel of freedom. We turn now to the person of Jesus, as he is portrayed in the New Testament literature, for here we see that Jesus himself is an "event of freedom," a freeing parable, as we might say. This is apparent in Jesus' peculiar relationship to tradition in its varied dimensions, viz., to the law, to piety, and to custom.

The Torah is the most formal representation of Jewish tradition, and it is here that Jesus' peculiar relationship to tradition is most clearly evident. The Jesus of the New Testament witness did not abrogate the law in any simple sense. Matthew 5:17 indicates this explicitly ("Think not that I have come to abolish the law and the prophets"), but it is also implicit in Jesus' *use* of tradition in order to go beyond it. Thus in Mark 2:23–28 Jesus appeals to tradition (i.e., to the precedent of David) in order to justify his departure from tradition regarding the sabbath. Jesus did go beyond the law, however, even if that transcendence was at the same time thought to be the fulfillment of the Torah's original intention. The clearest juxtapositioning of Jesus' teaching and the Torah comes to expression in the Sermon on the Mount. Six times in Matthew 5 Jesus says, "You have heard that it was said by men of old. . . . But I say unto you. . . ."

Had Jesus simply rejected the validity of the law, his opposition to it would have been less audacious, merely the substitution of one principle ("rejection") for another ("acceptance"). Precisely because he does honor the law (see Matthew 5:17–20) his departure from tradition in pursuit of the Torah's deeper meaning is a more radical form of freedom. In the Mark 2:27 saying ("The sabbath was made for man and not man for the sabbath"), Jesus does not elevate the importance of human need above that of tradition on the grounds that the tradition is worthless; rather, he elevates the importance of immediate human need vis-à-vis tradition in spite of his appreciation of that tradition. Jesus dares to revise a *worthy* past. In fact, Jesus sometimes breaks with his contemporaries by opting for a stricter rather than a more flexible application of the law.[10] The point is that Jesus is not bound to the stance of opposition. Because he is truly free from the law, he is free for the law as well.[11]

Peter Hodgson observes that Jesus' radical freedom with respect to the Torah "may be broadened" to include, too, his relationship to religious piety in general.[12] A quotation from Käsemann amplifies this point:

> The pious people of the time were deeply incensed by Jesus' association with sinners, tax-collectors, and prostitutes. To understand this rightly, we have to keep in mind the rabbinic axiom that the nation that does not know the

law is accursed. Nor should one forget that Pharisaism was a lay movement, which tried to bring as far as possible into everyday life the regulations for purification that were prescribed for the priests. The guiding ideal here was the priestly nation, which through its holiness would stand continually before God. Thus Jesus, through his associations, infringed not only a social and political taboo, nor even simply the prevailing moral order. He repeatedly violated what was regarded as God's will, and in so doing seemed to attack God the Father himself.[13]

Jesus' critique of piety is best embodied in his cleansing of the temple (see Mark 11:15-19). Clearly this action was not an attack upon piety per se, for its purpose was to purify a "house of prayer." Thus it was a pious critique of piety. Yet it was more. It was the subjugation of piety to justice—the money-changers were driven out because they were "robbers" and not simply because they were money-changers. For this reason, Jesus' action was, as Hodgson says, "a religious action with overtly political ramifications."[14] Piety is more than religious; it becomes ingrained in social and political structures. Thus Jesus' freedom from piety no less than for piety provoked a challenge that was political no less than religious and religious no less than political. It loosed unsettling repercussions with implications for the whole human order.

The remarkable freedom that Jesus embodied is also evident in his attitude toward custom (though it must be said that our distinction between custom and piety is as forced as that between piety and adherence to the law). This is especially true of his relationship with women. Jesus did not verbally challenge the customs pertaining to women, but his lifestyle in this regard was a dramatic challenge to the first-century conventions.[15] Jesus' love for Mary and Martha is in the Fourth Gospel accorded an importance (at least) equal to his love for their brother Lazarus (John 11:5). Jesus entered the house of these two unmarried women and talked with them about things that were ordinarily reserved for conversations among males. In response to Martha's complaint, Jesus approved Mary's neglect of her "feminine" chores while she listened to his teaching as any male disciple would have done (see Luke 10:38-42). John 4:7-30 asserts Jesus' audacious willingness to fraternize with a woman who was both a sinner and a Samaritan, an action that left his disciples astonished. In his parables, Jesus employed images from the everyday world of women, and in one parable a woman is used, it would seem, to represent God (see Luke 15:8-10). In his sayings, he attacked male lust, the deeper implication being the defense of female integrity—the personhood of a woman, as we would now say, is demeaned no less by her reduction to an object of lust than by adultery (Matt. 5:27-28). Women, some married and some single, left their homes and families to follow Jesus. They were apparently among his disciples from a fairly early period, traveling along with the twelve. They were present at his death—perhaps thereby risking their lives, some scholars believe. And it was to them that Jesus first appeared, according to the empty tomb traditions. Apparently, the centrality of women to Jesus' personal life was, from a historical standpoint,

> an unprecedented happening in . . . that time. . . . Jesus . . . knowingly overthrew custom when he allowed women to follow him. . . . Jesus was not content with bringing women up onto a higher plane than was then the custom; . . . he brings them before God on an equal footing with men.[16]

Whatever the decision of scholars about the historical authenticity of particular events and sayings recorded in the New Testament, there is no question that the "freedom of women," as we might put it, was a central element of the Jesus present to faith. In this respect, and in all of his speech and actions, Jesus meant freedom in the experience of the first believers. His tradition was affirmed yet re-ordered, his context creatively transformed. The coming kingdom that he proclaimed and already embodied was indeed, as Hodgson has said, the "kingdom of freedom."[17] And this freedom he bestowed upon others.

Jesus as the Gift of Freedom

The freedom Jesus proclaimed and personified was not his alone to possess. As we have already begun to see, his disciples and other hearers (some of them at least) experienced Jesus' gospel of freedom also as a gift of freedom. The gift had many facets, among them liberation, obligation, and responsibility.

FREEDOM AS LIBERATION

The freedom Jesus transmitted to others was, in part, a liberation from various forms of bondage. Often, no doubt, this liberation was fragmentary. Often it came to be refused after initial fascination. Yet it was such as to give rise eventually to a new community which broke open traditional restrictions of sex, class, piety, and even family.[18] "Who are my mother and my brothers? . . . Whoever does the will of God is my brother, and sister, and mother" (Mark 3:33, 35). Into this community coming to be free were gathered "not only 'tax collectors and sinners' (Matt. 11:19; 8:11), but also liberation fighters (Zealots), daylaborers (fishermen), women (a social outclass), foreigners (Samaritans), the poor and diseased."[19]

The character and significance of this liberating community is represented chiefly by the table-fellowship at which Jesus ate and drank with those "who had made themselves as Gentiles" according to the binding conventions of the time.[20] Nothing, Norman Perrin tells us, could have been a more outrageous affront to Jewish sensibilities. Moreover, nothing could have constituted a more blasphemous attack upon the predominant Jewish "theology" of the day, for this fellowship of the table was nothing less than a claim that this is the nature of the coming kingdom. "I tell you, many will come from east and west and sit at table with Abraham, Isaac, and Jacob in the kingdom of heaven" (Matt. 8:11). The coming reign of God, already being made present, is a classless community, free of the social, economic, and religious forms of bondage that we protect and seek to sanctify. It will be, and is, a celebration—"a glutton and a drunkard" these occasions prompted Jesus' critics to say of him (see Matt. 11:19)—in which destructive structures of human contrivance are abandoned for the joyous sharing of life's basic treasures.

It is impossible to deny the concreteness of the now-coming end-time, as it is represented by the Jesus of the Gospels. He was the bringer of physical healing, the breaker of social bondage, the celebrant of food and drink, no less than the agent of forgiveness. What could all of this mean, except "of such is the kingdom of heaven"? The still-ahead but already-coming liberation promises the fulfillment, not the abandonment, of the concrete dimensions of our existence. As we shall see again in Chapter Six, the kingdom even now being brought to completion is somehow inclusive of the material context of our lives. In it, the "physical" and the "spiritual" (as we commonly understand those terms) are together brought to a fullness of freedom.

If we are struck by the concreteness of the liberation being made present in Jesus, we are also surprised by its openness. The exchange between Jesus and Peter regarding Jesus' identity (reported in Mark 8:27–30: "Who do men say that I am?") almost certainly reflects the historical fact that even among his closest followers the question of Jesus' identity was not yet decided, not yet agreed upon. The fellowship of freedom Jesus offered to them did not have some particular belief about Jesus as its prerequisite. Neither was there such a requirement for the freedom from disease, illness, and even sin that Jesus bestowed upon others. As Willi Marxsen says, several times in the Synoptic Gospels Jesus attributes healing to the faith of the one healed, but that faith is never said to be faith in Jesus. Marxsen adds: "It is also quite striking that in these older traditions Jesus ascribes faith to individuals—even Gentiles— without first requiring of them a confession of faith."[21] Affirming who Jesus is, is not a prerequisite for beginning to participate in the liberated community. Jesus first offers the reality of freedom, at *whatever* point bondage is experienced. Then there arises in some form the question of Jesus' identity. The gift provokes the decision about the giver, not vice versa. Freedom's liberation is open to all.

FREEDOM AS OBLIGATION

The gift of freedom is experienced as obligation no less than liberation. The direction of freedom's obligation is lived out in Jesus' clear identification with the poor and the oppressed. This identification is implicit in the character of Jesus' proclamation and person, and in the community he created, about which we have already spoken. It is quite explicit, moreover, in several New Testament passages (see, e.g., Matt. 11:5; Mark 10:21; Luke 6:20f., 24f., 12:16–21, 16:19–31). For these reasons, Luke 4:18–19 is a particularly appropriate summation of the meaning of Jesus' ministry:

> The Spirit of the Lord is upon me,
> because he has anointed me to preach good news to the poor.
> He has sent me to proclaim release to the captives
> and recovering of sight to the blind,
> to set at liberty those who are oppressed,
> to proclaim the acceptable year of the Lord.

But if Luke 4:18–19 sums up the meaning of Jesus' ministry, and thus the nature of the obligation Jesus proclaims and embodies, Matthew 25:31–46 depicts freedom's obligation even more forthrightly. That obligation, as portrayed in this parable of the Last Judgment, is to serve the neighbor's need. It is conveyed by means of two equations. One is that of Christ and the neighbor: "As you did it to one of the least of these my brethren, you did it to me" (v. 40). Hence, to decide for the one sent to proclaim the release of the captive means to release the captive, and to decide against those who are hungry means to decide against Christ. The other equation emerges out of the fact that Christ is represented in this parable as the judge who "separates the sheep from the goats" (v. 32). In this judgment, one's own destiny, and thus the destiny of one's own freedom, is related to the freedom of the neighbor. Both equations show freedom to be of a piece—the source of freedom is tied to the extension of freedom; the freedom of one is tied to the freedom of all. Therefore, the experience of freedom implies the extension of freedom everywhere, in whatever form it is lacking. That is the obligation of the kingdom of freedom. The free community is free*ing*. The one who is being liberated is liberat*ing*.

The obligation integral to the freedom Jesus gives, as that obligation is portrayed in the New Testament, reveals the full continuity between Jesus' gospel and the Hebraic identification of "knowing (and loving) God" and "doing justice."[22] Earlier we noted this identification in Isaiah 58: "Is not this the fast that I choose: . . . to let the oppressed go free, . . . to share your bread with the hungry?" Jeremiah 22:13–16 makes the same point (with a more troubling specificity): "Woe to him . . . who says, 'I will build myself a great house with spacious upper rooms,' and cuts out windows for it, paneling it with cedar, and painting it with vermilion. Do you think you are a king because you compete in cedar? Did not your father eat and drink and *do justice and righteousness*? . . . He judged the cause of the poor and needy; then it was well. *Is this not to know me?* says the Lord" (italics added).

From every vantage point it is apparent that Jesus' gospel, and the obligation it entails, includes the pursuit of social justice. This raises the question of the political nature of Jesus' role: Is Jesus' freedom, and is freedom's obligation, political in nature? It would be as unhistorical to expect the New Testament Jesus to speak in the socio-political language characteristic of today as it would be to expect him talk about satellites and spatio-temporal relativity. But Jesus did seek to revolutionize human relationships in an absolutely fundamental way, something that can by no means be accomplished without forcing drastic changes in the religious/social/political system. The consequences, both personal and political, of Jesus' departure from the Law, his treatment of women, and his table-fellowship illustrate this point. The best example, however, is probably his cleansing of the Temple (Mark 11:15–19 and parallels).[23] We can readily see that this action—simply a concrete "doing" of the gospel—was "political" in the broad sense of that term, affecting as it did the corporate structures of human life. However, the evidence is strong that the action was perceived by Jesus' contemporaries to be "political" in the narrower sense of that term, as well. The Sadducees, in response to Jesus' action, moved to "destroy him" (v. 18); for this purpose they sought the aid of the Romans, against this man who had "stirred up" the people "throughout all Judea" (Luke 23:5). Only a political threat would have concerned the Romans. To be sure, Pilate (according to Luke 23) attempted, first, to shift the case to Herod's jurisdiction and, secondly, to find Jesus innocent as charged. But never is there any denial that the charge itself was political in nature. The final bit of evidence, of course, is Jesus' crucifixion, an execution reserved for political criminals.

Our varied considerations lead to a single conclusion: Jesus' gospel directly affected the political sphere. In view of this, the saying regarding what is God's and what is Caesar's (Mark 12:17 and parallels) can hardly be taken to mean that "God" and "politics" are unrelated. It is probable that the temptation of a purely "political messiahship" was strong during Jesus' ministry, and that it was firmly rejected, but it by no means follows that what God demands is indifferent to the social and political order.[24] To know God is to do justice; to serve Christ is to release the captive. Mark 12:17, thus, is better understood as a warning against *reducing* what belongs to God to what belongs to Caesar. Jesus' role is not simply political, not simply reducible to the political options of a particular historical epoch. But it is applicable to such options, for its revolutionary impact upon human relationships did then and would always challenge unjust political and social orders to their very foundations. The already coming kingdom does not only demand social and political change, but that, too, is a part of its obligations. To decide for or against the kingdom of freedom is also to decide for or against this obligation. The change of heart it requires is a decision for freedom in *all* of its forms.

FREEDOM AS RESPONSIBILITY

We have said that the gift of freedom in Jesus is experienced as liberation and as obligation. But it is more. This additional dimension may be represented by the term "responsibility," a term which gains its meaning, however, in relation to Jesus' authority.

The New Testament claims that Jesus spoke and acted with a peculiar sense of authority. Mark expresses this by saying that Jesus went into Capernaum and "on the sabbath he entered the synagogue and taught. And they were astonished at his teaching" (1:21–22a). Mark does not say what Jesus taught, as if that were not the main point. The point is the manner of his teaching: "for he taught them as one who had authority, and not as the scribes" (v. 22b, cf. v. 27). In Mark, especially, Jesus' authority is exemplified in healing stories (particularly accounts of exorcisms), stories used liberally to illustrate Jesus' authoritative power over the forces of sickness and evil. But the clearest claim to special authority is implicit in Jesus' forgiveness of sins. When Jesus says to the paralytic in Capernaum, "Son, thy sins are forgiven," the shocked scribes wonder "in their hearts, 'Why does this man speak thus? It is blasphemy! Who can forgive sins but God alone?' " (Mark 2:5–7 and parallels). The claim to the power to forgive sins provokes such a response because this power is the ultimate expression of authority, in first-century Judaism; it is "doing what is God's prerogative."[25] This is true in the strongest possible sense, for, in certain New Testament traditions at least, when the issue of authority is raised, Jesus does not authenticate his action by appeal to the will of God. In Mark 11:27–33 (and parallels) Jesus is asked to reveal the basis of his authority. By way of reply, Jesus asks his questioners to identify the authority of John's baptism. They say they do not know. Curiously, Jesus answers: "Neither will I tell you by what authority I do these things" (v. 33). One is led to ask whether there lies behind this cryptic reply the audacious claim that Jesus' authority is, in a sense, not God's but his own!

The assumption that Jesus' authority is claimed to be *his* authority helps to account for the inclination in the New Testament to associate Jesus with God. This inclination begs to be accounted for because there is ample evidence that Jesus distinguished himself from God. He spoke of God as his father, which suggests extraordinary intimacy,[26] but also distinctness; he distinguished his will from that of God; he prayed to God; and in reference to his youth, Jesus is said to have "*increased* in wisdom . . . and *in favor with God* and man" (Luke 2:52, emphasis added). In the face of such persistent distinctions, what is the basis of the strong urge to identify Jesus and God in a special way? Perhaps the answer—whether it became apparent before or after the resurrection experience does not matter—lies partly in the consciousness of Jesus' audacious claim to act, not for God or even in God's place (which would still preserve the distinctness of God and Jesus), but rather to act, from a Jewish standpoint, *as God alone would act.* For the early believers this meant either that Jesus was indeed a blasphemer, as charged in Mark 2:7 and 14:64, or else he was one with God in some unique way.[27] Only if the latter were true could his forgiveness of sins fail to be blasphemy.

We need not evaluate the earliest Christian understanding of Jesus' authority, nor do we need to evaluate the early explanations of the "oneness" of Jesus and God taken to be implied by Jesus' authority. The point here is this: Jesus' claim to authority is a claim to act from out of himself; it is a claim to freedom. In this connection, Peter Hodgson writes:

> The term *exousia* does not mean "authority" in the sense of an authoritarian tradition or law, inherited privilege, physical coercion, or power. Rather it means "freedom" in the sense of "freedom to act" or "original freedom," a freedom . . . usually found in conflict with "tradition," which replaces originality with . . . legitimation. . . . Jesus' *exousia* was expressed in his conflict with the legal and cultic tradition of Israel. He came forward as a teacher with disciples, occasionally argued in rabbinic fashion, and allowed himself to be addressed as "rabbi." Yet he was independent of the scribes, belonged to no school, and founded none. The Evangelists expressed this as follows: ". . . he taught them as one who had *exousia,* and not as their scribes." . . . He introduced a new mode of speaking and teaching—original, not derived, internally authoritative rather than dependent upon external tradition.[28]

If the New Testament claims for Jesus a peculiar freedom in the form of his authority even to forgive sins, it also suggests that Jesus transmits that authority, that freedom, to his followers. In the controversy over the healing of the paralytic of Capernaum, the issue is Jesus' authority to forgive sins (Matt. 9:6 and parallels). Matthew carries the extraordinary commentary: "When the crowds saw it, they were afraid, and they glorified God, who had *given such power to men*" (9:8, emphasis added). The power in question is not Jesus' ability to heal; it is his authority—this is what was given "to men." This suggestion, that the authority of Jesus somehow becomes a possibility for human beings generally is also evident elsewhere. Matthew 18:18 and John 20:23 both represent Jesus as conferring this power on his disciples. Paul instructs the Corinthians to "deliver . . . to Satan" the man living with his father's wife (1 Cor. 5:5), as he himself delivers others "to Satan" (1 Tim. 1:20). Finally, insofar as the healings manifest Jesus' authority, the same suggestion may also be found in the statement that the disciples shall do even greater things than Jesus had done (John 14:12).

The fact that the passages we have cited serve primarily to vindicate orders of ecclesiastical authority (for which reason the passages from the Gospels are usually viewed as products of later tradition) does not counter the claim being made. The early tradition was dominated by the memory of the free Jesus who gives that freedom to others. The passages cited indicate that the authority ingredient in Jesus' freedom was experienced as a part of that gift no less than was liberation and obligation, even if that authority was interpreted along narrowly ecclesiastical lines. If such an interpretation restricts the meaning of the authority Jesus gives to all, it does not distort that meaning. The authority of freedom is the responsibility to order the structures of the world, including those of the church in the world.

Jesus' authority is his contextual creativity, i.e., his power to act out of himself, radically remaking the context to which he is nevertheless gratefully indebted. It is his power to "name the animals," in the tradition of Genesis 2, to order and reorder the forms of life in freedom for freedom. Jesus' example, as reflected in the early Christian witness, shows the comprehensiveness of that authority, its relevance to all dimensions of life. The good news, the release, the recovery, the liberty he proclaimed and embodied (see Luke 4:18–19) was always directed toward bondage as it was experienced. Usually bondage comes to awareness first at the most simple, basic levels—hunger, illness, powerlessness, and the like. Overcoming these basic forms of captivity was as central to the outworking of Jesus' authority as was the conquering of guilt and separation from God. That is why, in Matthew 25, the decision for the Jesus of freedom can be equated with the decision against hunger, thirst, nakedness, and imprisonment. This is not to say that estrangement and guilt—what *we* think of as being the "spiritual" forms of bondage—are less important. The forms of freedom are interrelated. The authority that seeks freedom's fulfillment begins *wherever* bondage is most vividly evident in order to bring awareness, reconciliation, and wholeness.

The gift of Jesus' authority is not his authority *over* others so much as it is his authority *for* others. It is their agency, their ability to respond creatively in the world, their responsibility. It is thus not a new law, the same structure of obligation filled with a new content; it is a new kind of law. It does not impose restrictions upon freedom; it articulates what is necessary in order that freedom be preserved and enhanced. The commandment to love God and the neighbor illustrates this, for it is a commandment to preserve freedom by nurturing its divine and human context, a warning against the forms of pride and sensuality that destroy freedom from without and within. The believer, therefore, experiences Jesus' authority as the command to live the life of freedom, to become a steward of freedom in the world, to reorder the world on behalf of freedom. The authority of Jesus is bestowed upon others as responsibility.

Jesus as the Power for Freedom

The freedom Jesus gives is in one sense a natural capacity, one which we already possess. It is that essence of human nature given in creation, the realization of which all human beings long for when they glimpse themselves truly. It is an essence, however, that is treated with equivocation at best. It comes as a gift, but it wears heavily upon the human soul, threatening our settled security.[29] Thus the treasure comes to be experienced as a curse. Anxious, we are tempted by the false security of pride or sensuality. We yield. Powerless before our own fear, we find ourselves unwilling and thus unable to take on the freedom that Christians see in Jesus. But Christian faith asserts that, somehow, Jesus empowers us, translating the abstract possibility of freedom for all into a real possibility for us. The Jesus who embodies freedom, and calls us to its gifts and tasks, makes possible our acceptance of it. To faith, Jesus is somehow the power for freedom. But how?

FREEDOM AND THE FORMS OF BONDAGE

There have been several Christian explanations of the power for freedom that Jesus is said to convey. The reason for this variety is simple: Christians have conceived of human bondage in different ways and their accounts of Jesus' power over bondage have therefore differed accordingly. This is already evident in the New Testament record of the earliest traditions. The first conception of how Jesus enables freedom was developed in dialogue with the heritage of Judaism. In this circumstance, human bondage was viewed as coming through the law; this was how the earliest Christians experienced bondage, even though bondage was not held to be the law's original purpose. Jesus brought freedom by overcoming the law that binds, a matter we discussed earlier. This theme is especially apparent throughout Matthew, the Gospel most clearly attuned to Jewish traditions and sensibilities. The Gospel of Mark, by contrast, was compiled for Greeks. For this reason it assumed more of a Hellenistic understanding of the impediments to freedom, communicating Jesus' power to bring freedom in the terms of this conceptuality. The powers of bondage are represented by the demonic forces that control the earth. Jesus' power for freedom is his victory over these spirits, a victory somehow finalized by the cross, according to Mark.

These two understandings of bondage, and their corresponding views of Jesus' power for freedom, are both reflected in the theology of Paul. Paul says that we are bound by both the law and the cosmic powers of sin and death. We cannot suppose, however, that this is to be taken as some final synthesis, inclusive of all the possible accounts of bondage and Jesus' power over it that are appropriate to every time and place. For one thing, aspects of some accounts extant in Paul's own time do not fit nicely into Paul's system. Paul's account does not fully coincide with or include the theology of Luke-Acts, for example, in which the cross plays no crucial salvific role as it does in Mark and Paul. Neither is the view of Hebrews adequate to the Pauline experience of bondage. In Hebrews, Jesus is the power of salvation simply because he is the "model" of salvation or, in our terms, of perfect freedom. For the bondage that Paul experiences, however, one needs more than a model; one needs some outside act of liberation before it is even possible to follow the model of freedom.

It may be that Paul's account of the requisites for freedom seems more adequate to us than does the account in Hebrews. But if so, that is because our experience of captivity is more like that of Paul than the writer of Hebrews. In any case, the point is that one must not accept as the authoritative starting point some preconceived notion of the nature of bondage, even if that notion is sanctified by tradition. What is decisive is the actual experience of bondage characteristic of the milieu in which one lives. This, in fact, was the point of Paul's departure. Paul, born a Jew and called to preach to the Gentiles, sought to articulate a view of bondage which expressed the modes of experience he contacted and to some extent shared. Paul rejected the notion that he should first "convert" the Gentiles to a view of captivity dependent upon specifically Jewish sensibilities, even though these sensibilities were integral to Paul's personal self-understanding, before formulating for them the message of Jesus' freeing power (see Gal. 2). Paul allowed the mode of bondage experienced by his hearers to form his account of *how* Jesus brings freedom. His account was relative to the situation. But *that* Jesus enables freedom was the "absolute," the claim applicable to all forms of bondage. In becoming "all things to all men" (1 Cor. 9:22) Paul expressed in whatever manner the context required the Gospel that Jesus frees. He became "*as* a Jew" and "*as* one outside the law," a Gentile (1 Cor. 9:20–23, emphasis added), in order to proclaim in the terms suitable to their particular views of the world the Gospel variously available to all.

Paul's method of proceeding is the only one appropriate to a theology for freedom. A theology for freedom from *our* bondage must begin with an analysis of our bondage, captivity as it is experienced by us. This means, in the first place, that a description of unfreedom is to be validated, not by its conformity to some authoritative notion of the enslaved experience (not even Paul's notion), but rather by its adequacy to our experience of captivity, reflectively considered. Hence the description of elements of bondage given in the previous chapters is not to be accepted simply because it parallels the witness of tradition. It would be wrong, of course, to suppose that our present experience is divorced from the tradition that contributes so overwhelmingly to it. It would be wrong also to think that our tradition can in no way deepen our present self-understanding. Indeed, the judgment that tradition does enrich and illumine our analysis of bondage today motivated the structure of the two preceding chapters. Nevertheless, the account of unfreedom's nature is to be deemed valid, if at all, because it rings true to our reflective experience of our own enslavement as humans in this time and place.

Following Paul, we must begin with bondage where we are, not where Paul or someone else was or is. This means, in the second place, that our description of the power for freedom grows up out of our experience of being liberated from the things that bind us. Again, understanding our tradition is fundamental to understanding ourselves; the present is grounded in the past it contains. But the definitive, and in that sense binding, Christian assertion is *that* Jesus frees us. The description of *how* that liberation comes through Jesus is not defined by the past, however importantly the past informs it; the description emerges out of the reality for ourselves no less than for others, of being made free. If it is in dialogue with, and under the critical eye of, the past that we come to speak of Jesus as the power for freedom, it is nonetheless we who speak and our topic is the Christ who is present as the power for freedom to us today.

THE CROSS AS THE DESPAIR OF FREEDOM

The most striking thing to us about the Jesus of the New Testament witness is the confidence of his freedom. He acts on his own audaciously, yet he is serene in the certainty that his freedom is affirmed by the Father. Jesus assumes the role reserved for God alone, in his forgiveness of sin, for example. Instead of fearing the wrath of heaven, however, he speaks to God as "Abba" (Mark 14:36), the most intimate form of the address, "my Father." Jeremias has shown that "Abba," which conveys an unsurpassable sense of confidence and security, is not known to have been used at all in Judaism, but it was always used by Jesus.[30] Jesus takes on the responsibility of full freedom, totally confident that his doing so is fully in accord with things as they ultimately are. His human freedom incarnates the divine freedom; the messiah of freedom reveals fully the will of the God of freedom. This claim is clear in the New Testament witness.

It is also clear, however, that Jesus came to look upon his death as more than the prospect of agony and defeat, as more even than a test of his willingness to die for freedom. He experienced death as forsakenness: "My God, my God, why hast thou forsaken me?" (Mark 15:34 and par.). Whether this quotation from Psalm 22 represents the spoken words of Jesus or is a product of the early tradition, it can hardly do other than to reflect the actual experience of the death of Jesus as witnessed and remembered in the community of faith. Jesus' sense of forsakenness cannot be explained away. After its experience of the risen Lord the Church would come to view the cross differently, but apart from that experience the death of Jesus could only mean divine abandonment, the despair of freedom.[31] God, in forsaking the messiah of freedom, seemed to have forsaken freedom itself and thus, too, had God forsaken the divine character. The gospel of freedom has been denied by the former God of freedom. Human bondage, to the law, to the demonic powers—however human bondage is experienced—it is victor after all.

Jesus' sense of forsakenness must be affirmed. Not only does the New Testament insist upon it; it is also demanded by our unsentimental experience of freedom. In our discussion of sin we saw that the situation of our denial of freedom is the anxiety that freedom's exercise brings. We do not "like" being free. Freedom brings the burden of insecurity. We fear it, and unsure of freedom's ultimate worth, we shun it. We hide from ourselves the creativity of freedom, succumbing to the dictates of the context about us. This is the sin traditionally known as sensuality. Or we deny the contextuality of freedom, pretending that freedom has no intrinsic limits, interdependence, responsibility. This tradition has been known as the sin of pride. In either of these forms, sin is our lie about ourselves, it is untruth. But we prefer the security of that self-deception to the anxiety of freedom.

Apart from the resurrection, the death of Jesus means that freedom's affirmation is groundless. Anxiety is the curse of freedom and bondage is its solution. The messiah of freedom is dead. Death itself—physical mortality—does not mean defeat, as we saw in the last chapter. It is the ultimacy and irreversibility of bondage accomplished in death that is the defeat of freedom. But Jesus' death is defeat in another sense, for it means God's abandonment of the freedom Jesus embodies and proclaims. The absolute confidence of Jesus' freedom is a mistake. God has not confirmed Jesus' freedom. God has forsaken Jesus. The messiah of freedom is dead. So, too, is the God of freedom. The God of bondage reigns. This, apart from the resurrection, is the meaning of the cross in a Christian theology for freedom.

THE RESURRECTION AS THE CONFIRMATION OF FREEDOM

One of the ironies of modern biblical scholarship lies in the fact that it began, in the nineteenth century, assuming that historical investigation would reveal the resurrection event to be a secondary accretion contributed by tradition. Within a few years higher criticism, with admirable honesty, admitted the need for quite an opposite conclusion, namely that belief in Jesus' resurrection lay at the heart of the earliest traditions about Jesus. The same scholarly methods, however, also found two different traditions attesting to the resurrection. One is the appearance tradition, expressed particularly in the writings of Paul; the other is the empty tomb tradition, contained in the Gospels. Few, if any, scholars doubt that the appearance tradition is the earliest and in fact the only one based directly on an eyewitness account. This eyewitness account, of course, is Paul's own testimony, especially in 1 Corinthians 15. There Paul says that Jesus was raised on the third day and he appeared at various times to a list of persons of whom Paul was the last. That passage, presumably amplified by accounts of Paul's primarily auditory experience of the risen Lord in Acts 9, 22, and 26, furnishes the earliest description of the resurrected Jesus.

Paul himself discussed the nature of the resurrected reality in 1 Corinthians 15:35ff. Although he is here speculating on the nature of the resurrected body in general, it is clear that Paul takes the resurrected reality of Jesus as his model. Paul's description centers around the polarity of continuity and discontinuity. The sense of discontinuity is conveyed in a juxtaposition of categories such as physical and spiritual, perishable and imperishable, mortal and immortal. Yet the discontinuity is not absolute, for resurrection is said to be a transformation of the first set of categories into the second. As Paul writes, *"this* perishable nature must put on the imperishable, and *this* mortal nature must put on immortality" (v. 53, italics added). The point is, first, that resurrection is not viewed as an astounding phenomenon somehow significant in itself, perhaps because of its very oddity; resurrection is important because of what it does, because of the transformation that it brings about. Secondly, resurrection is not seen as a disembodied spiritual reality set over against the present order of our lives; resurrection transforms *this* present, embodied existence.

From some conceptual perspectives at least, the witness of the empty tomb tradition is implicit in the appearance tradition. If, for example, the physical body is conceived as a self-identical, material object that endures continuously throughout a portion of space-time, and if Jesus' risen reality is the transformation of his physical body, then the resurrection appearances would indeed entail the empty tomb. Of course, even in this view the empty tomb would have no intrinsic religious significance; the fact that someone's body is resuscitated would be unusual, but it would have no unavoidable religious meaning. The empty tomb would be the presupposition, in this particular worldview, of the more important Christian assertion that Jesus' concrete, embodied reality is, in its relevance to faith, somehow radically transformed. The essential Christian claim about the resurrection is *that* this transformation has taken place. The way the transformation is explained—i.e., *how* the resurrection occurred—will of necessity vary according to the cosmological presuppositions from within which the resurrection is experienced.

For a Christian theology for freedom, as developed in this book, the crucial claim of the resurrection may be put this way: Jesus as the embodiment and proclamation of freedom is, in spite of his death, made real by God to the believer as the one who reflects God's essential character, whose audacious freedom God approves, and whose call to freedom's fulfillment reveals God's insistent will for persons everywhere. The essential point is *that* God confirms the freedom incarnate in Jesus.

How God's confirmation of Jesus' freedom is conveyed in the resurrection experience could conceivably have more than one speculative explanation, even within the context of a process understanding of reality (though, in the nature of the case, no explanation can *prove* from some neutral standpoint the veridicality of such an experience). Significantly, however, in Romans 4:17 resurrection and creation are equated, suggesting thereby the unprecedented novelty of the resurrected reality for which illuminating analogues are lacking. The underlying insight of this equation is perhaps the judgment that such speculation is futile. Perhaps speculations about the nature of the resurrection are indeed useless, either because there are several possible explanations, or because—due to its uniqueness—there are none. In any case, they are in most circumstances of dubious theological value. The theological claim is that God's confirmation of freedom's worth is made a reality for the believer.

Jesus is the power for freedom because his resurrection is the experience of God's affirmation of freedom. The connection between this "affirmation" and "power" is not a logically necessary one. One could be empowered solely from within to do that which has no ultimate worth, or one could be helpless to do that the value of which is irrefutable. But there is much to commend the claim that, in fact, the ultimate condition of freedom is, in the long run at least, the confidence that somehow freedom is grounded in the nature of things.[32] This claim, I believe, expresses a judgment fundamental to Christian faith. As Niebuhr observes, in the biblical view anxiety is rooted in unbelief, that is, in the lack of faith or trust in God.[33] Romans 11:17–25 suggests this by comparing unbelief to the separation of a branch from the sustenance of the tree's root system. And Matthew 6:31–32 makes a similar point when it bases Jesus' injunction, "do not be anxious," upon the assurance that "your heavenly Father knows." Our reflections presuppose the truth of the same judgment: freedom can flourish only when it is rooted in the confidence of freedom's abiding worth.

The resurrection is the assurance that freedom's worth has an immutable basis in the character of God. The confidence of freedom is confirmed. The faithful God has affirmed the freedom of Jesus. The messiah of freedom is the Lord of freedom, he whose cause endures throughout all time by virtue of the persistent power of God. Thus, the resurrection "inaugurates a liberative future."[34] It is that which impels the Christian to defend and extend freedom in every place, in every form, for every person.

In the reality of the resurrection, Christians come to understand the cross differently. The cross is not God's abandonment of freedom; it is God's "abandonment" of an impassible security.[35] It is incarnation without reservation, for in the cross God shares fully, at one with Jesus, the pain of freedom's betrayal by the world. Not abandonment, but God's suffering faithfulness to freedom everywhere is now evident in the cross. Jesus' cross, thus, is for Christians the decisive manifestation of God's universal commitment to freedom. With this new understanding of the cross, faith is able to affirm that wherever freedom suffers, God, too, shares fully its loneliness, pain, and death.

If the God of freedom suffers at the hands of bondage, we have revealed here not only God's faithfulness but also something of freedom's destiny. A freedom that loves the world and seeks its release is unwilling to accept the world as it is, to let the world rest happily in its captivity. This is freedom's world, to be sure, the world fashioned by the God of freedom for its realization. But the homeland of freedom is dominated by powers of bondage to which freedom can never give assent. Thus freedom is homeless in its own homeland, at war, in a sense, with its own country.[36] Because of the God it serves, a persistent freedom must continually suffer the pain and hostility of alienation. This is what a faithful freedom, human and divine, must endure. But if so, what may freedom hope for?

Notes

1. Beginning in this way is not to imply that it is historical research, whether into the "historical Jesus" or into the "apostolic witness," which stipulates the content of Christian faith. The historian's task is to make judgments about the verbal and other forms through which the Jesus present to faith has been fallibly but efficaciously witnessed to in various historical periods. On the assumption that in the witness of others we may encounter the Jesus to whom witness is made, the results of historical study are a basic resource, though they are not as such normative, for theology. In the very nature of the case, empirical findings cannot be normative for faith, or, therefore, for theology, which is disciplined reflection upon faith. The content of faith, and thus its final norm, is conveyed through lived realities that transcend (though they certainly *may* include) the endeavors of historical scholarship.

A discussion of the methodological standpoint presupposed in this study, and especially in this chapter, will be published separately. A partial indication of the viewpoint to be defended may be gleaned from my essay, "What Is a Christian Theology?" in Harry James Cargas and Bernard Lee, eds., *Religious Experience and Process Theology* (New York: Paulist Press, 1976), pp. 41–52, *if* that essay is viewed through the corrective perspective provided in the final paragraphs of Chapter Two of the present work.

2. From R. Schnackenburg, *God's Rule and Kingdom* (New York: Herder and Herder, 1963), p. 13; cited in Norman Perrin, *Rediscovering the Teaching of Jesus* (New York: Harper & Row, 1967), p. 55. Cf., too, the discussion of this point in Jon Sobrino, *Christology at the Crossroads* (Maryknoll, N.Y.: Orbis Books, 1978), pp. 42–46.

3. See Hans Conzelmann, *An Outline of the Theology of the New Testament* (New York: Harper & Row, 1969), pp. 106–15, and *Jesus* (Philadelphia: Fortress Press, 1973), pp. 68–77; Günther Bornkamm, *The New Testament: A Guide to Its Writings* (Philadelphia: Fortress Press, 1973), pp. 10–15; Joachim Jeremias, *New Testament Theology: The Proclamation of Jesus* (New York: Scribner's, 1971), pp. 96–108; Norman Perrin, *The New Testament: An Introduction* (New York: Harcourt Brace Jovanovich, 1974), pp. 288ff., and *Rediscovering the Teaching of Jesus*, pp. 54ff.

4. William A. Beardslee, "Uses of the Proverb in the Synoptic Gospels," *Interpretation* 24 (January 1970): 61–73.

5. Robert W. Funk, *Language, Hermeneutic and the Word of God* (New York: Harper & Row, 1966), p. 126.

6. See Perrin, *Rediscovering the Teaching of Jesus,* pp. 82f.

7. Peter Hodgson, *New Birth of Freedom: A Theology of Bondage and Liberation* (Philadelphia: Fortress Press, 1976), p. 228.

8. Cf. Hodgson's discussion of the intention of the Parables of the Good Samaritan and the Great Supper in terms of freedom, in ibid., pp. 229ff.

9. William G. Doty, *Contemporary New Testament Interpretation* (Englewood Cliffs, N.J.: Prentice Hall, 1972), p. 123.

10. Ernst Käsemann, *Jesus Means Freedom* (Philadelphia: Fortress Press, 1970), pp. 23f.

11. Our interpretation of the nature of Jesus' freedom in general, and with respect to the Torah in particular, is not dependent upon the claim that this freedom is historically unique. David Daube (in *The New Testament and Rabbinic Judaism* [London: Athlone, 1956], pp. 55–62) and others have argued against the conclusion that the relation of Jesus to the law, as portrayed in the New Testament, is without historical precedent in Judaism.

12. Hodgson, *New Birth of Freedom,* p. 233.

13. Käsemann, *Jesus Means Freedom,* p. 28.

14. Hodgson, *New Birth of Freedom,* p. 234.

15. The uniqueness of Jesus' attitude toward women is generally acknowledged. In the following paragraph, however, I am largely dependent upon Paul K. Jewett's book, *Man as Male and Female* (Grand Rapids: Eerdmans, 1975), pp. 94ff.

16. Joachim Jeremias, *Jerusalem in the Time of Jesus* (Philadelphia: Fortress Press, 1969), p. 376.

17. Hodgson, *New Birth of Freedom,* pp. 227ff., 276ff., and passim.

18. Dorothee Soelle, *Political Theology* (Philadelphia: Fortress Press, 1974), pp. 65f. Cf. Leonardo Boff, *Jesus Christ Liberator: A Critical Christology for Our Time* (Maryknoll, N.Y.: Orbis Books, 1978), pp. 282–86.

19. Hodgson, *New Birth of Freedom,* p. 223.

20. On the significance of the table-fellowship, see N. Perrin, *Rediscovering the Teaching of Jesus,* pp. 102–108; Günther Bornkamm, *Jesus of Nazareth* (New York: Harper, 1960), p. 81; and J. Jeremias, *New Testament Theology,* pp. 115ff.

21. Willi Marxsen, *The New Testament as the Church's Book* (Philadelphia: Fortress Press, 1972), p. 88.

22. See Gustavo Gutiérrez, *A Theology of Liberation* (Maryknoll, N.Y.: Orbis Books, 1973), pp. 195ff.

23. On this see William R. Wilson, *The Execution of Jesus* (New York: Scribner's, 1970), pp. 97ff.

24. J. Jeremias, *New Testament Theology,* pp. 71f.; L. Boff, *Jesus Christ Liberator,* p. 60.

25. Bornkamm, *Jesus of Nazareth,* p. 81. The power to forgive sins is also claimed implicitly in the actions of Jesus, such as his table-fellowship. On this, see J. Jeremias, *New Testament Theology,* pp. 114ff.

26. See Jeremias, ibid., pp. 61–68, and *The Prayers of Jesus* (Naperville, Ill.: Allenson, 1967), pp. 11–65.

27. Käsemann, *Jesus Means Freedom,* p. 25.

28. Hodgson, *New Birth of Freedom,* pp. 225f. Here Hodgson is following Kurt Niederwimmer, *Der Begriff der Freiheit im Neuen Testament* (Berlin: Verlag Alfred Topelmann, 1966), pp. 4, 165–66. The essential points to be made here are (a) that

Jesus' authority is an element in the New Testament witness, and (b) that in this witness the authority of Jesus serves to clarify the nature of the freedom Jesus is said to embody and bestow. These points are not dependent upon the additional judgment that such a claim to authority is unique and unprecedented, an historical judgment apparently accepted by Hodgson (and Niederwimmer) but disputed by others (e.g., David Daube, *New Testament and Rabbinic Judaism,* pp. 205–210).

29. See the discussion in Chapter Four.

30. Jeremias, *New Testament Theology,* p. 66; see also note 25, above.

31. Generally speaking, this interpretation of the cross appears also in the liberation Christology of J. Sobrino; see *Christology at the Crossroads,* pp. 179–235.

32. See A. N. Whitehead, *Adventures of Ideas* (New York: Free Press, 1967), pp. 67f. Lowell G. Colston cites several empirical studies which show that love or affirmation is essential to creativity. (See Colston's "Love and Creativity" in Harold H. Anderson, ed., *Creativity and Its Cultivation* [New York: Harper, 1959], pp. 172–84.) The relevance of Colston's contention to our thesis is evident in view of the intimate connection of creativity and freedom, pointed out in Chapter Two of this book.

33. Reinhold Niebuhr, *The Nature and Destiny of Man* (New York: Scribner's 1955), Vol. I, p. 252.

34. Sobrino, *Christology at the Crossroads,* p. 263; cf. 259–271.

35. The fullest development of this theme in contemporary theology is Jürgen Moltmann's *The Crucified God* (New York: Harper & Row, 1974), pp. 200–278.

36. Rubem Alves' exploration of aspects of freedom's homelessness is moving and perceptive throughout *Tomorrow's Child: Imagination, Creativity, and the Rebirth of Culture* (New York: Harper & Row, 1972).

Chapter Six

The Future of Freedom:
An Understanding of Salvation

The centrality of the kingdom of God in the gospel's witness to Jesus was noted in the last chapter. There we saw how the kingdom of God may be viewed as the kingdom of freedom because Jesus means freedom in his word and in his being. In this view, freedom promised and freedom (coming to be) possessed may rightly be said to be the content of the kingdom. In the development of Christian belief, however, the form of the kingdom, especially in its relationship to human history, came to have a profound effect upon the understanding of the meaning of the kingdom. The form of the kingdom of God in Christian thought distorted the meaning of the content of the kingdom.

We shall first briefly examine the way in which an inadequate conception of the relationship of the kingdom of God to history emptied the idea of freedom, and thus the kingdom of freedom, of any concrete, human meaning. In the following section we will trace the effort in modern theology to restore the kingdom of God to its proper relationship to history, an effort that comes to fruition in the work of Third World and minority liberation theologians. Benefiting from this work, we shall attempt in the final section to develop a fuller account of the relationship of human salvation, represented by the theme of the kingdom of God, to human history. Our own constructive efforts, driven by the analysis of the preceding chapters, may deviate somewhat from the specific conclusions of these liberation theologians to whom we are so much indebted. Yet, our intent is to preserve their intent, to express in a different culture and through a different conceptuality that same biblical confidence in a God who, in our history and "by the power at work within us, is able to do far more abundantly than all that we ask or [even are yet able to] think" (Eph. 3:20).

The Abandonment of Hope for History

Scholars agree that the Jesus of the very earliest New Testament witness proclaims the kingdom of God as future, yet also as now coming into the present. Norman Perrin writes, "Certain events in the ministry of Jesus are nothing less than *an experience* of the Kingdom of God."[1] But Perrin adds that this "fulfillment in the present, although it is truly fulfillment, still only anticipates the consummation in the future."[2] Or as Robert Funk states the relationship, "The new reality of the kingdom is surprisingly present and yet it belongs to the future."[3] However, Funk goes on to argue that neither "present" nor "future" are to be understood in a strictly chronological sense:

> The tension between present and future in the proclamation of Jesus is not adequately understood if it is expressed as the highest possible degree of imminence. It is not a matter of an interim between sign and reality, however brief that interim is, but a matter of the coincidence of the two modes of temporality. . . . The kingdom is so near that it completely overwhelms and dominates the present; the kingdom can no longer be looked for, awaited. So long as the kingdom is anticipated in a chronological sense, it is still possible to view the coming of the kingdom from a distance. But for Jesus this is impossible. He therefore transcends the question of time as such. If one still asks about the date, it is only because he has misunderstood the signs. Whether one fixes the date near or far, the question has been converted into an apocalyptic question.[4]

None of this is to say, of course, that Jesus' message was not thoroughly eschatological, i.e., fundamentally oriented toward a divine action yet to be accomplished. Like the prophets, Jesus proclaims the kingdom as rooted in "a future act of God which will be decisive for the salvation of the people in a way in which his past acts on their behalf were not."[5] The point seems to be that this future is more than that which is not yet; it is that "not yet" which somehow stands already (and always?) at the cutting edge of the historical present, determining its reality and its direction. Hence, if one asks when God's future is coming, one has missed the point of *God's* future. It alone is the "not yet" that already is in our history, without ceasing to be that which still is coming to transform our history.

If the above interpretation of the form of the kingdom in Jesus' message is correct, it is apparent that Christianity soon moved to other ways of conceptualizing the relationship of the kingdom of God to history. The reasons for this change are unclear. Perhaps it was in part the intrinsic difficulty of the notion of a future that both is and is not, the notion that seems to characterize Jesus' message in the earliest portrayals. Or perhaps the change was prompted by a changing conceptual milieu and the need to communicate the gospel in the terms of this new reality. In any case, apocalypticism, a particular form of the eschatological vision, had come to dominate the first-century mind, and the manner in which the kingdom is related to human history in the work of the New Testament writers is pervaded by the categories of an apocalyptic eschatology.

Apocalypticism seems to have emerged with force a century or two before the turn of the Christian era.[6] Like its broader expression, Jewish apocalypticism saw the world gripped in a battle between two cosmic forces, God and Satan. Now captive of the powers of evil, the world is soon to be freed by the imminently dawning day of God's judgment and salvation. The end of the old age is near; current events reveal that the Messiah approaches. Satan's forces are breaking out in one last demonic convulsion, but God is preparing to act. This was the apocalyptic vision.[7]

Debate continues about the timing of apocalypticism's entry into Christianity.[8] It is agreed, however, that this entry was early enough for the apocalyptic outlook to become the "controlling factor" of the New Testament literature, especially the Synoptic Gospels.[9] The result was a simple historicizing of the kingdom of God, with history being divided into two "times."[10] The time of Jesus, in this view, had been a time of feasting in the presence of the bridegroom, but now the bridegroom has been taken away so that the present is an interim of fasting and expectation. The Messiah will return in the near future, however, and bring with him the final redemptive event. Only the faithful are able to discern the signs revealed during the days of Jesus which substantiate this expectation. With the coming consummation, though, the Messiah will be exalted and that which is now known only to the faithful will be made plain for all to see. For the present believers must remain steadfast in their servanthood and humiliation, separated from the world and confident in the assurance that soon those who are now last, by the standards of the present, will be first in the kingdom of God.

Even if Jesus' message of the kingdom was not itself apocalyptic,[11] one can hardly conclude that the apocalypticizing of his message in the New Testament literature was entirely inappropriate. Whatever apologetic reasons might have led to the adoption of apocalypticism as a vehicle for expressing the meaning of Jesus, there is also the plain fact that this outlook did preserve much of that understanding of the kingdom reflected in the very earliest traditions about Jesus, or what scholars identify as Jesus' own understanding of the kingdom. Even if the vision of apocalypticism and that of Jesus were differently expressed, the existential reality or experiential grasp of life that they both produced may well have been much the same. For both the future was experienced as being crucial to the present—the present was in ferment precisely because of the inbreaking of the future, and the present crisis was a time of decision on behalf of that inbreaking future. For both the kingdom expected was historical; it had to do in one form or another with the renewal of this world in all its dimensions. But there was also a difference. For Jesus, apparently, the coming future could never be said to be "now" and "here" in the conventional sense of these terms, even though it was emphatically not a kingdom to be realized in some other world. Apocalyptic Christianity obscured this wise ambiguity. Its expected "not yet" was simply chronological, a hope to be realized in tomorrow's here and now. The result, as we shall now see, was that hope in its purely historicized, apocalyptic version became vulnerable to the fatal threat of an uncooperative history.

Apocalyptic eschatology intensified and came to dominate Christian expression until well into the second century. Standing in the tradition of

Jewish apocalypses such as Daniel, the Relevation of John, written about
A.D. 90–100, vividly foresees the imminent end of the world's present
captivity.

> Now war arose in heaven, Michael and his angels fighting against the
> dragon. . . . And the great dragon was thrown down, that ancient serpent,
> who is called the Devil and Satan, the deceiver of the whole world—he was
> thrown down to the earth. . . .

> And I saw a beast rising out of the sea, with ten horns and seven heads. . . .
> And to it the dragon gave his power and his throne. . . . Also it was allowed to
> make war on the saints and to conquer them. And authority was given it over
> every tribe and people and tongue and nation, and all who dwell on earth
> will worship it, every one whose name has not been written in the book of life
> of the Lamb that was slain. . . .

> Then I saw heaven opened, and behold, a white horse! He who sat upon it is
> called Faithful and True, and in righteousness he judges and makes war. . . .
> And the armies of heaven, arrayed in fine linen, white and pure, followed
> him on white horses. From his mouth issues a sharp sword with which to
> smite the nations, and he will rule them with a rod of iron; he will tread the
> wine press of the fury of the wrath of God the Almighty. . . .

> And I saw the beast and the kings of the earth with their armies gathered to
> make war against him. . . . And the beast was captured, and with it the false
> prophet who in its presence had worked . . . signs. . . . These two were
> thrown alive into the lake of fire that burns with brimstone. And the rest
> were slain. . . .

> Then I saw a new heaven and a new earth; for the first heaven and the first
> earth had passed away, and the sea was no more. And I saw the holy city, new
> Jerusalem, coming down out of heaven from God . . . and I heard a great
> voice from the throne saying, "Behold the dwelling of God is with men. He
> will dwell with them, and they shall be his people, and God himself will be
> with them; he will wipe away every tear from their eyes, and death shall be
> no more, neither shall there be mourning nor crying nor pain any more, for
> the former things have passed away."

> And he who sat upon the throne said, "Behold, I make all things new" (from
> Chapters 12, 13, 19, and 21).

The apocalyptic hope, beautifully illustrated by this passage, was not
treated kindly by the events of history, however. The heavens never
opened, the white horse never appeared; tears, death, mourning, and
pain were never wiped away. So by the middle of the second century
another voice—one anticipated by Luke-Acts and by the Gospel of
John—was being heard, a voice expressing hesitancy about the imminence of the coming of the kingdom. This voice is best represented in the

New Testament by 2 Peter, dating from around A.D. 150. It suggests that Christ is postponing his return because of his compassion for the lost; he is giving to all an opportunity to repent and be saved. The delay of the coming of the kingdom seemed to substantiate the logic of this argument.

Finally, in the third and fourth centuries the more hesitant voice became the voice of orthodoxy. Christians settled down for an indefinite stay in the world of present bondage. Origen, in the first half of the third century, presented the kingdom not as an historical reality coming in space and time so much as an event in the souls of believers. What stirred his "profoundly Hellenic imagination," to use Norman Cohn's apt description,[12] was the notion of individual spiritual progress begun here but completed in a life beyond this world. By the time of the early church Fathers, the kingdom of God had little to do with a hope for history. Those eschatological expectations not realized in the form of the Church on earth were attached to the destiny of the "spiritual" self, the separate soul in its salvation from this world. To the extent that unrealized hope remained at all, it was thoroughly divorced from history.[13]

Apocalyptic expectation by no means died out with the developments described above. It lived on from time to time in the fervent piety of the oppressed masses, sometimes coming to tumultuous, even violent expression. But it was to remain an underground expectation carefully muted by official statements of belief. The reasons for this official neglect are obvious. Christianity was now the religion of the Empire; the Church was a prosperous power in the world. Its official representatives, thus, saw little to gain by the dramatic reversal envisioned in apocalyptic expectations. And there was a less self-serving reason for the official disapproval of apocalypticism. In the past, apocalyptic hopes plainly had been *un*fulfilled. Given this history of consistent disappointment, only fools could continue to believe that the expectations of their own time would be realized, when every generation before had hoped for naught. For this reason, especially, the experienced reality of apocalyptic anticipation was now internalized, depoliticized, and made narrowly spiritual. This means, also, that it was withdrawn from history.

The early Christian hope which, following Judaism, had longed for the renewal of persons in the totality of their relationships—physical, social, political—became a Hellenized longing for the eternal future of the soul in separation from its body and its world. To be sure, the two visions could coexist to some extent, and they did. The language of each found a place in theology and piety. But the Hellenized hope for a separate soul's salvation gained effective primacy over the biblical anticipation of God's coming transformation of *this* world. A new Jerusalem, a new heaven and earth, a created world set free from its bondage to decay and death—these became verbal icons for the edification of the masses. More sophisticated expectations were directed toward the individual's destiny, the unity of the invisible soul with the ineffable God. Thus, Christian hope was made safe from defeat. It could not be disappointed by history because it sought nothing in history or for history—only salvation from history.

The Recovery of Hope for History

In view of the foregoing discussion, we can imagine the shock and consternation of the theological world when, around the beginning of this century, Johannes Weiss and Albert Schweitzer announced in effect that the apocalyptic sectarians were right.[14] Weiss and Schweitzer showed conclusively that the Jesus of the New Testament was neither a modern theologian nor an orthodox Christian. He was, they contended, thoroughly apocalyptic in his outlook. Even if subsequent scholarship has backed off from their claim about the apocalypticism of Jesus, it has uniformly confirmed the eschatological character of Jesus' message and the apocalyptic nature of the early Christian view of Jesus' meaning.

The destiny of this discovery from Weiss and Schweitzer on is interesting. The discoverers, Weiss and Schweitzer, disowned their discovery, eschatology in general and apocalypticism in particular, embracing all the more firmly their respective versions of the ethical religiousness of nineteenth-century Protestant liberalism. It was Karl Barth who dared, in 1921, to restore eschatology to the center of Christian reflection: "If Christianity be not altogether and unreservedly eschatology, there remains in it no relationship whatever to Christ."[15] Yet so tightly did Barth embrace eschatology that he squeezed it out of history altogether into a transcendent realm that stood equidistant from all points in time. The expected kingdom, or *parousia*, does not take "place in *any* time, because it is . . . the basis and eternity of *all* times."[16] The eschatological hope in Barth had nothing to do with the future renewal of this life and the transformation of this world; its object is a transcendental reality that breaks into history at every point. Eschatology is transcendentalized, and history is thereby emptied of its "historicness," its quality of going somewhere. The "destiny" of history enters each moment of history from beyond.[17]

Rudolph Bultmann also affirmed the eschatological character of Christianity. He, too, removed eschatology from history, not to the transcendence of eternity but to the inner, subjective reality of existential decision. The eschatological reality is the human decision which in response to the proclamation of the Word of God says "yes" to the possibility of a "concrete encounter" with one's neighbor, in which alone one finds "true history."[18] Bultmann held that Jesus' proclamation "does not envisage a future to be molded within this world. . . . It only directs man into the Now of this meeting with his neighbor."[19] In Bultmann no less than in Barth, the eschatology that emerges has little if any of the historical dimension that characterized the message of Jesus in the earliest New Testament witness or the hope of later Christian apocalyptic.

Finally in the 1960s, mainline Christian theology came to affirm, without equivocation of intent, the historical character of Christian hope. Jürgen Moltmann, Johannes Metz, and Wolfhart Pannenberg were the central figures in this development, though Moltmann's *Theology of Hope* proved initially at least to be its basic document.[20] Christian hope is historical hope, Moltmann says, because God is the Lord of the human future, not of some eternal present. God is the one who "confronts us with a promise of something new and with the hope of a future given by God."[21] In the Old and New Testaments, Moltmann shows, these "promises enter into fulfillment in historical events, yet are not completely resolved in any event, but there remains an overspill that points to the future."[22] Thus, while preserving the historical intent of apocalypticism, Moltmann avoids its traditional naiveté by refusing to identify the promised kingdom with any particular historical achievement, any particular "here" and "now." This is a point to which we shall return.

Moltmann holds that for Christian faith the central promise of that which is new is the resurrection.[23] Christian faith "sees in the resurrection of Christ . . . the future of the very earth on which his cross stands. It sees in him the future of the very humanity for which he died."[24] Thus the resurrection is itself the new that is promised; it is the injection into the historical process of the radically new future that is to come. For this reason, Moltmann speaks of the resurrection as the "*novum ultimum*," a creation *ex nihilo*.[25] And, therefore, although the resurrection is a "foretaste" of the coming kingdom, it is such a foretaste only as promise, not as fulfillment.[26] Because of its utter novelty, the nature of the resurrection is "hidden."[27] Thus also hidden is the nature of the human future that it is said to embody.

Moltmann's insistence upon the absolute novelty of the resurrection seems to derive from his affirmation of God's absolute autonomy. This, in turn, grounds Moltmann's confidence that history is not bound by the oppressive possibilities that now define its limits. From the reality of a totally new event in history, the resurrection of Christ, Moltmann argues to the possibility and guarantee of a totally new human future.[28] The promised future is to be given by God, not by the past. Yet this particular way of preserving hope for history also "guarantees," it would seem, a historical dualism that undermines the significance of *our* history. The coming world is totally discontinuous from the existing one. Moltmann writes:

> The sole Lord of the kingdom is the God "who has raised Jesus from the dead" and therein shows himself to be the *creator ex nihilo*. His kingdom can then no longer be seen in a historic transformation of the godless state of man and the world. His future does not result from the trends of world history. . . . This makes it impossible to conceive the kingdom of God . . . as a result of world history.[29]

The future of this world is to be created "out of nothing," not out of the present. As Moltmann states the relationship, this future would seem to be "our" future only in the peculiar sense that it might be said to occupy some spatio-temporal region that lies as a successor to our historical advance. This future is to come "after" the present, but not in any sense "from" the present. This odd separation of world history from "its" coming future produces an immobilizing separation of present action from future achievement. The entirely new future must be entirely in God's hands. Consequently, there can be no connection between what humans do in the world and what God can accomplish for it. The coming kingdom, supposedly the future of our very earth, is something we "can only await in active hope."[30] The activity of our hope, however, is merely anticipatory, not constitutive of the coming future. There is no "causal relationship between [our] historical activity and the construction of the eschatological kingdom."[31]

It is clear that Moltmann wishes to affirm the *historical* character of the kingdom. If he fails, or if his success is only partial, the cause is not the weakness of his intention so much, perhaps, as the lingering dualism of the tradition upon which he depends. This, at any rate, is the judgment of Third World liberation theologians with respect to European political theologies such as Moltmann's.

Protestant and Catholic theologies have consistently separated human action from divine achievement. In Catholic thought, since the sixteenth century, this took the form of a distinction between nature and supernature.[32] Salvation was seen to be a gift of divine grace entirely. Inasmuch as the consequences of human activity, occurring in the realm of nature, are "earned" by that activity, they were held to be indifferent (if not deleterious) to the gift of salvation. They may, in the degree of their effort and their God-directed intent, be evidence of the gracious bestowal of divine merit, and in this way human activities may be relevant to one's eternal salvation. But the salvific consequence is not the natural result of the action nor is it related to the result of the action. The consequence of human action has nothing to do with the accomplishment of God's saving purposes. Salvation is a divine act of grace, occurring in the realm of supernature. Each human act, thus, may have two types of consequences; the one which is earned is of merely temporal significance taking place in the realm of nature, the other of saving significance is a gift of grace in the realm of supernature. This dualism gave rise to others—the eternal and the temporal, the sacred and the secular, the Church and the world, the priesthood and the laity, etc.—and to multiple perversions of each.

Protestant dualism dates from Luther's doctrine of the two kingdoms or two realms.[33] Luther began with an affirmation of the absolute perfection of God which he contrasted with the imperfection of every human achievement. From this there followed the inability of the human will to do the good and the inability of human society to embody the good. Salvation, a free gift of divine grace, is an achievement of the heavenly kingdom where liberty and justice in a "spiritual" sense are available to the elect through faith alone. Human effort produces the kingdoms of this world. Here injustice and bondage are socially necessary and individually inevitable. Here rulers are entitled to "hit, stab, kill" in order to keep the oppressed in their places.[34]

European political theology, Catholic and Protestant, moderates these dualisms by locating the coming kingdom in the future of this world. There is, so to speak, a single spatio-temporal order in the future of which God's kingdom will be achieved. Following tradition, however, the divine achievement still is viewed as being totally independent of all human effort. "*God himself,*" Rudolf Weth writes, "brings about the revolutionary action that is decisive for the *coming* of his kingdom. His action cannot be effected or replaced by *any human action.*"[35] Thus, a dualism of agency remains, and only God's activity effects the kingdom. The result of this view, we have noted, is: first, a coming kingdom so fully discontinuous with this world that it is the future of *this* world only in a very odd sense, if at all; and, secondly, the irrelevance of all human action with respect to the advent of the kingdom. However unintentionally, the worth of this world and of our human efforts in it are both undermined by this theological position.

Contemporary liberation theology offers an account of the kingdom of God that is genuinely historical.[36] Its central tenet is the essential oneness of the historical process, a oneness that effectively defuses the dualisms of traditional theology. Gustavo Gutiérrez expresses this tenet when he writes that "salvation is an intrahistorical reality . . . [which] orients, transforms, and guides history to its fulfillment. . . . The history of salvation is the very heart of human history."[37] The liberating process through which the kingdom of God is coming into being is *in* history. The achievement of the kingdom is the fulfillment of history, the history of *this* world. Leonardo Boff writes:

> The Kingdom of God is not only spiritual, but also a total revolution of the structures of the old world. Hence it is presented as good news for the poor, light for the blind, healing for the lame, hearing for the deaf, freedom for those in prison, liberation for the oppressed, pardon for sinners and life for the dead (cf. Lk. 4:18–21; Mt. 11:3–5). It follows that the Kingdom of God is not the other world, but this world transformed and made new.[38]

The unequivocally historical nature of the kingdom and its coming, in liberation theologies, is demonstrated by the bold ease with which utopian and Christian hopes are spoken of together. Boff says that "the Kingdom of God expresses man's utopian longing for liberation from everything that alienates him . . . and not only man but all creation."[39] Rubem Alves passionately defends Christian utopianism—the confidence that "somehow, somewhere, God is . . . overthrowing the existing order"—as over against the Christian realism that has dominated the North American scene.[40] Gutiérrez, holding that the gospel and utopianism imply each other,[41] says that utopian projection is an integral part of the historical process of liberation, which process is the "growth of the Kingdom."[42]

Liberation theologians insist that the kingdom of God is coming, and will be, *in* history. They do not, however, simply identify the realization of the kingdom with the liberating processes of history. Gutiérrez' distinctions on this issue are representative. He holds that liberation is a single phenomenon with three different levels of meaning.[43] There is, first, the level of economic, social, and political liberation. Secondly, there is the process of cultural liberation in which human beings come to understand themselves as agents of their own futures. Third is liberation from sin, which is the root of all forms of bondage, and admission into communion with God. The full process of liberation is not identical with any particular event or level of events because it encompasses all of them on every level, material, cultural, and spiritual.

Precisely because liberation is viewed as an all-inclusive reality, however, it is distinguished from particular events and processes not only as the whole of which they are parts but also as the source of judgment in terms of which they are evaluated. The kingdom is therefore said to be present in history both as denunciation and annunciation.[44] Referring to its negative mode of presence, denunciation, Segundo writes that the kingdom is a guard against "a degeneration into inhuman rigidity or stagnation or a tendency to sacralize the existing order."[45] Others make essentially the same point.[46] Yet all are quick to point out the positive function of even a negative judgment. If the kingdom of God transcends every social, political, and personal reality, thus revealing the inadequacies of all, it nevertheless provides a perspective in terms of which some historical achievements are seen to be relatively better than others. Every negation implies an affirmation; every "thou shalt not" suggests a "thou shalt." Consequently, the desacralizing presence of the kingdom is not uniform; some imperfections are revealed to be better than others. It is the kingdom's presence in history that makes possible our imperfect discriminations among history's imperfections.

One such discrimination is Juan Luis Segundo's claim that in the contest between capitalism and socialism, Christianity must unequivocally side with those political systems "in which the ownership of the means of production is removed from individuals and handed over to higher institutions whose concern is the common good."[47] Segundo does not minimize the dangers of human fallibility in making judgments about signs of the kingdom's coming. But neither does he believe that fallibility requires, or even allows, Christian neutrality with respect to particular historical developments, a tendency liberation theologians see implicit in European political theologies.[48] The Christian's judgments can be quite wrong, Segundo acknowledges, but this was no less true of the pronouncements of the prophets, whose mistakes are now a matter of record. Should the prophets have remained silent, Segundo leads us to ask, because they were fallible?[49]

Segundo also knows that, even if correct in a general sense, a human judgment (such as his preference for socialism) cannot amidst the contingencies of history guarantee the realization of that which it envisions. Even if socialism is preferable to capitalism, to illustrate the point, the Christians of Latin America cannot be sure that their particular socialist experiments will succeed. And why should certainty be expected of them? Segundo asks. He writes: When their critics require

> Latin Americans to put forward a project for a socialist society which will guarantee in advance that the evident defects of known socialist systems will be avoided, why do [they] not demand of Christ also that before . . . [healing a sick man], he should give a guarantee that the cure will not be followed by even graver illnesses.[50]

Should Jesus never have attempted healings because he sometimes failed altogether (Matt. 13:58; cf. Mark 6:5) or because those he healed eventually became ill and died anyway? Why, then, do we, worried by the uncertainties of the future, warn against the risky venture of identifying and serving the healing processes of liberation because in one way or another the venture may fail?

Annunciation, the positive presence of the kingdom, is not only manifested in the reality of relative goods, in the writings of liberation theologians. One finds in their work a willingness to say that there is in history an authentic, if only momentary, realization of that coming kingdom which is fully good. Annunciation is more than promise, more than approximation; it is the inbreaking of the kingdom itself.

To be sure, the distinction between approximation and realization is not systematically developed by liberation theologians, but again and again it presses forward in their reflections. Leonardo Boff writes:

> The Kingdom of God . . . [is] not already complete, but it has been inaugurated. It is present among us (cf. Luke 17:21; 11:20) in Jesus himself and in the new praxis which he initiated and which is open to the future. The parables . . . speak of the future which is nevertheless fermenting in the present. There is no separation between present and future, but a process of liberation.[51]

Similarly, Enrique Dussel identifies the Church, when it is involved in the "movement of liberation," as the "sign of the eschatological forward movement of the Kingdom"; the Eucharist, Dussel tells us, is "a foretaste" of the kingdom, a "feast of liberation."[52]

The Christological overtones in such passages are significant. They reflect, if only in a general way, the Christological formulations of tradition. During the fourth century, Arius, an Alexandrian presbyter, held that the *ousia*, or substance, of the Son, though the highest of all the creatures, is nevertheless different from and lower than that of the Father. The Council of Nicaea (325) rejected this, asserting that the Son is of the same divine substance or nature as the Father.[53] With a similar logic, liberation theologians seem to be maintaining against an "eschatological Arianism" that the foretaste of the kingdom in history is not an approximation, not even the highest approximation of the kingdom; it is a manifestation of the very essence of the kingdom itself. The parallel with traditional Christology, however, may be pushed even farther. In 451 the Council of Chalcedon affirmed that the full divinity and full humanity of Jesus were united in his own person "without division, without separation."[54] There is a similar nondualistic intent in liberation theology's view of the kingdom. The kingdom of God is not a mystic reality distinct from concrete history. In its coming, the kingdom is fully united with the pain and joy of earthly existence—"without division, without separation." "The praxis of Jesus Christ is the Kingdom itself already present."[55]

We have seen that liberation theologians, beginning with a doctrine of the oneness of history, hold that the kingdom of God is coming *in* human history even if it is not completely realized in the historical events of this process. The kingdom is present as denunciation and as annunciation. Its realization, though never the whole of the kingdom, is fully the presence of the kingdom and fully at one with the realities of human history. It remains for us to add only that, for liberation theology, the coming of the kingdom depends in part upon human action.

The essential character of the human contribution to the coming of the kingdom of God—our "freedom to construct the kingdom"[56]—is clearly asserted by liberation theologians. "A liberating event," Segundo writes in reference to historical occurrences, "derives . . . a genuinely causal character with respect to the definitive Kingdom of God."[57] Although he acknowledges the temptation toward legalism implicit in traditional Catholic theology, it has, Segundo says, one justification: "However shakily, it does try to preserve the principle that human liberty is liberty for something definitive and indeed eschatological: the building up of the kingdom of God."[58] Drawing upon an analysis of the Exodus, Gustavo Gutiérrez, too, explicitly affirms "the liberating and protagonistic role of man . . . [as] coparticipant in his own salvation."[59] Yet in every case these theologians couple this type of affirmation with an equally clear assertion of God's essential role in the process of liberation whereby the kingdom comes.[60] The two affirmations are most clearly held together—even if they are never clearly connected, a point to which we shall return—by Rubem Alves, who calls the creation of freedom a "joint enterprise" of God and humanity,[61] one which cannot be based upon "the powers of man alone."[62] After maintaining the necessity of preserving both divine grace and human creativity, Alves says:

> Grace creates the possibility and necessity of man's action. Man is a co-creator. The pact between God and man means that God waits for what man can give to the new tomorrow. The pact means that God, in the fulness of his eternity, needs, longs, and waits for man. "There is something essential that must come from man" in God's future, Friedman comments. . . . In this context the words of the apostle which otherwise could sound so confusing acquire a new meaning: "Work out your own salvation with fear and trembling; for God is at work in you."[63]

In its insistence that we are co-creators of the coming kingdom of God, liberation theology undoubtedly departs from the language of most Christian eschatology. In our very different conceptual world, however, this departure at the level of language is necessary if we are to preserve the central *intention* of traditional eschatology, which is to proclaim that God's kingdom will mean the renewal of *this world*. *My* future self, if indeed it is mine, must in some measure be continuous with and contributed to by my present self. Similarly, the future of this world must be at least partially affected by its past; any future reality that is not somehow contributed to by the present is not the future of this world. As we noted in Chapter One, the ancient mind generally viewed human action to be a *reaction* to the pre-established "nature of things" and therefore inessential to it. Human action had no essential relationship to reality, the "way things are," present or future. In the modern worldview, on the other hand, and certainly in any theology for human freedom, the exercise of freedom is a constitutive part of the world's present reality. It follows that, for us at least, human action in the world now has a constitutive relationship to the future of this world. The characteristic way in which human action is related beyond itself is through its causal efficacy. Human action "makes a difference" to its future. For this reason, any future that is truly said to be the future of this world, which includes our human action, must in some measure be affected—enriched or impoverished—by the exercise of our human freedom. The future of this world includes the future of our action in this world. Thus, the contemporary insistence upon the "causal character" of human action for the coming kingdom is for us unavoidable if we are faithfully to proclaim the ancient confidence that the kingdom of God is indeed to be *this* world's future.

In liberation theology the biblical vision of salvation as the renewal of heaven and earth—"the whole creation" (Rom. 8:22)—finds its restoration.[64] Not since its loss in the fourth century, when the apocalyptic version of this vision was "officially" suppressed, has the fully historical character of salvation been so resolutely affirmed. Even so, it is perhaps *affirmed* by liberation theology more adequately than it is clarified. By liberation theologians we are told that God's action and ours constitute one history, yet God's transcendence over history is also referred to, leaving us to wonder about the relationship of history and God. We are told that God's kingdom is historical, yet its transcendence over every individual event and all of them together is also affirmed, leaving us to wonder about the "location" or ontological status of the kingdom in relation to history. We are told that the kingdom is a consequence of human effort, yet its character as a gift of grace is also cited, causing us to ask about the relation of God's agency and ours. We are told that history is a closed continuum of cause and effects in terms of which the hope for renewal is unrealistic, yet the realism of hope due to God's infusion of new possibilities into history is affirmed, making us wonder about the relationship of divine action to natural causality.

None of the paradoxes we have mentioned are to be attributed to all liberation theologians. Neither is the value of their work vitiated by the presence of such paradoxes where they do occur. The point is that in addition to the welcomed breadth of their vision of salvation and their courageous application of this vision to their own concrete circumstances, there is also, if only secondarily, a need for more systematic reflection upon the meaning of that to which they give witness. Gustavo Gutiérrez says that theology is "critical reflection on Christian praxis in the light of the Word."[65] We mean only to suggest that such a witness to the Word will be strengthened if, in its "critical reflection," a socio-economic and cultural analysis is supplemented with a search for greater conceptual clarity. Gutiérrez himself recognizes this point. With respect to his "one history" doctrine, he writes: "Contemporary theology has not yet fashioned the categories which would allow us to think through and express adequately this unified approach to history."[66]

The conviction underlying the final section of this chapter is that the categories of Whiteheadian process thought enable us to express the power of a Christian vision of salvation in a manner that is conceptually adequate. Philosophical categories enable us to say what might be; they do not, however, empower us to seek one or another of those futures that are shown by philosophical analysis to be possible. For the Christian, it is God's confirmation of freedom in Christ that transforms an abstract possibility into a moving vision. The Christian vision, as liberation theologians proclaim, is of a future of this world to which freedom's faithful struggle makes a difference. The promised kingdom represents the fulfillment of the work of freedom, both human and divine. To a systematic consideration of what this means we now turn our attention.

The Hope for Freedom in History

Christian apocalyptic preserved a hope for history. Its flaw, we have seen, was its reduction of the expected kingdom to a particular historical achievement. Such a hope was doomed, partly because history so frequently refuses the possibilities for which hope longs. But it was also doomed because hope for the kingdom of God seeks more than is possible in any one circumstance. A single historical achievement actualizes some values but not others. All the values represented by the kingdom of God are not simultaneously possible. The finest achievements of history are real goods to be cherished and nurtured, but one of the values of every historical accomplishment is that of uncovering other values not yet actualized, perhaps not yet even envisioned. The apocalyptic dream of an infinitude of value realized in a finite historical moment is self-contradictory.

The alternative and eventually orthodox hope that came to dominate Christianity after the fourth century fell prey to its own version of illogic, as we have also noted. In order to escape the refutation of history, it sought the fulfillment of history in a non-historical event, variously interpreted. But an "end" of history that is *non*-historical is indeed an *end* of history, not its fulfillment. Whatever values may be ascribed to such a reality, they cannot include the values accruing to the historical character of the temporal process. Orthodox Christian piety, it would seem, has intuited this point; its disdain for history—however much theology itself has sought to moderate that disdain—is the inevitable consequence of a hope for the non-historical "fulfillment" of historical reality. Regardless of its expressed intention, non-historical hope promises the annulment of history, not its salvation.

Both versions of hope, apocalyptic and non-historical, commit another mistake. They ignore the theological consequences of the infinitude in God's nature. Jürgen Moltmann sees the problem clearly, even if he fails to follow out its implications. Speaking of the realization of God's promises in history, Moltmann writes:

> Man's hopes and longings and desires, once awakened by specific promises, stretch further than any fulfillment that can be conceived or experienced. . . . Hence every reality in which a fulfillment is already taking place now, becomes the confirmation, exposition and liberation of a greater hope. . . . *The reason for the overplus of promise* and for the fact that it constantly over-spills history *lies in the inexhaustibility of the God of promise,* who never exhausts himself in any historic reality but comes "to rest" only in a reality that wholly corresponds to him.[67]

Moltmann puts "to rest" in quotes, indicating, one supposes, his awareness of the difficulty of such a notion. A God whose promises are inexhaustible or infinite cannot come "to rest" without thereby betraying the divine fecundity, the divine potential for the realization of further value. And a God, such as that of Christian faith, whose commitment is to the realization of this potential in and through the world, cannot bring history to rest without betraying the fecundity of history. An end to history is incompatible with the "inexhaustibility of the God of promise."

THE TIME OF FREEDOM'S FULFILLMENT

If we are to be faithful to the Christian view of God and the salvation God promises to history, we must "demythologize" the concept of history's fulfillment. Alfredo Fierro, the Spanish Catholic theologian, observes: "While it has freed itself from myths dealing with the beginning [of history, Christian theology] . . . has not freed itself from myths dealing with the final end of it all."[68] It must be added that demythologizing the end of history should not mean eliminating the future expectation from the Christian vision; rather, it should mean making the hope for history's fulfillment truly historical. A guide for doing this is provided in the ambiguity—a "wise ambiguity," we have called it—characteristic of Jesus' view of the time of the kingdom, as that seems to be represented in the New Testament (see pp. 108–10 above). The kingdom of God is somehow already here but also still coming. This distinction between present and future, however, is not simply chronological. The kingdom is both present and future, though not because it is "stretched out" over both modes of time. In some way, the kingdom is a "not yet" that already exists in the "now" without being identical to the "now."

The intention of this conception, we may suggest, is that the kingdom of God represents the reality of the redemptive potential of every historical accomplishment. The kingdom is a dynamic reality, not a static one. It is not a particular state of affairs to be achieved once and for all time, in history or beyond it. The kingdom is a divine, yet historical reality that calls every present into a richer and fuller accomplishment of its own distinctive possibilities for redemption. Thus, the kingdom is always present, as the fragmentary realization now of the present's own richer potential, and as the ideal that now beckons the present toward the pursuit of that potential. And the kingdom is always future, as the fulfillment of every present yet to be achieved.

The "time" of the kingdom, its relationship to the temporal present and future, may be clarified by reference to what in Whitehead's philosophy is called a "proposition." Whitehead distinguishes two basic types of reality, actuality (or the realm of "actual entities") and potentiality (or the realm of "eternal objects" or possibilities). But Whitehead adds that there is a curiously hybrid kind of reality that is not simply actual but neither is it simply a possibility; it is a combination of both. This type of entity is called a proposition. The "subject" of a proposition, Whitehead says, is some realized actuality as mere "food for a possibility," a "bare 'it' among actualities."[69] The "predicate" or "predicative pattern" of a proposition is a complex possibility, unrealized in fact, yet wedded by feeling and by vision to the actuality at hand. Propositions are present, both because they are real now and because they refer to what now is real. But they are also intrinsically tied to the future, uniting as they do the present with a potential for its own becoming. As Whitehead says, propositions are "the tales that . . . might be told about particular actualities"[70]—e.g., the present world without its hunger, hate, and inequity, without guilt and alienation, *this* world made new.

A proposition may be a statement, but it is not simply a statement; it may be felt, but it is not merely a feeling. A proposition has an objective status in the nature of things, for Whitehead, that secures its nagging aspirations in the cosmic process. These aspirations may be trivial or important, relatively impotent or powerful. They may contain the seeds of destruction. But they may also embody, for each particular age, the vision of its own redemption. Such, we are suggesting, is the kingdom of God. It is the human world as it should be in the divine mind.

In each age the kingdom of God is the "not yet" of fulfillment that already exists in the "now." Even though it is present to each present actuality, it is not identical to that state of affairs. Instead, it calls the "now" beyond itself to what it might become. Thus the kingdom is historical. It is historical, first, because it is dynamically changing, as is history itself. The kingdom is historical, secondly, because it is in history and about history, its "subject" being each present historical achievement and its "predicate" being that achievement's redemptive possibilities. In every historical epoch, in every moment, the kingdom is that particular actuality joined with "the tale that might be told" of its consummation.

We may now see how a genuinely historical conception of the kingdom of God is faithful to an affirmation of freedom's worth. The kingdom does not denote a fulfillment that somehow transcends freedom or brings freedom to an end. The kingdom represents the conjunction of every particular freedom and its redemptive promise. The kingdom represents the concrete fulfillment of our concrete freedoms. Thus freedom is not of penultimate worth, to be superseded by another more real mode of existence. Thus the service of freedom is not of merely extrinsic value, to be justified only by the greater value it promotes. The kingdom is not beyond freedom. The hope of the kingdom is a hope for freedom. The goal of the kingdom is freedom's growth and preservation. The place of the kingdom is the place of freedom, namely, in history. The Christian hope is for the fulfillment of our freedom in our history.

THE FOUNDATION OF FREEDOM'S FULFILLMENT

Christian hope for the future of freedom in history cannot ignore the arguments of those who, in the name of realism, condemn such hope as a baseless illusion. The most powerful critique of historical optimism in recent times has come from the quarters of Christianity itself, in the work of Reinhold Niebuhr.[71] Actually, Niebuhr acknowledges progress in history, even to the point of saying, for example, that it is "impossible to set any limits upon the brotherhood which may be achieved in history."[72] But

Niebuhr also shows how regularly progress is undone by regress, and how consistently the new goods that do remain are matched by new levels of evil.

History's resistance to a lasting balance of progress is due, in Niebuhr's view, to the persistence of inordinate self-interest in individuals and in collectives. The search for progress is always betrayed by our exaggerated estimates of the perspectives from which we view things. The free self which partially transcends nature also supposes itself to transcend other selves, even if ever so slightly. Likewise with groups of people: forces for social justice, such as movements for liberation, are in the end "always involved in the same idolatries as the forces against which they contend."[73] Niebuhr argues that all person have in varied ways thought of themselves more highly than they ought; that this trait has with considerable regularity been most destructively present when it was most cleverly disguised and most studiously denied; and that, therefore, we "ought" (theologically) to assume the persistence of these phenomena within ourselves. Finally, he shows, we are never able to transcend the finitude of our own perspectives sufficiently to be reliable judges of our own virtue; only one who completely transcends the limitations of finite perspectives can adequately gauge our moral advances, if such there be.

Niebuhr's sober estimate of the human prospect, though drawing heavily from the most profound traditions of Christian anthropology, appeals in the last analysis to the evidence of history. Again and again Niebuhr shows that the historical record gives scant encouragement to hope. And whatever one thinks of certain of its details, Niebuhr's estimate of historical progress can hardly be faulted in any of its essential respects. But if this is so, how is it possible to give a basis for that hope for freedom in history which we have found to be at the heart of Christian faith?

Liberation theology restored Christian hope to history by returning to the biblical conception that "history is one."[74] If, expanding on its lead, we return as well to the biblical notion that all reality, historical and natural, is one under God, it is possible to place the evidence Niebuhr gleans from history in a broader context. If nature and history are fundamentally unitary in their explanation, however diverse they are in degree, we can then look to the usually slow, sometimes cataclysmic, often wasteful, but genuine advance of the natural process for a better understanding of freedom's potential in history.

Niebuhr found this suggestion to be unacceptable for what are basically metaphysical reasons. A sharp distinction between nature and history, he argued, "is required by the uniqueness of human freedom in the historical process."[75] Ironically, however, Niebuhr's nature/history dualism reflects the modern, Western consensus more than it does the biblical understanding of the fundamentally unitary character of the creatures and the rest of creation, and thus of history and nature. And, significantly, this modern dualism is no longer necessary—indeed, it is probably no longer possible—in view of the organismic understanding of reality advocated in various forms of recent philosophical reflection. The philosophy of Whitehead, as we indicated earlier, provides us with one of the most influential of these nondualistic perspectives.

According to Whitehead, the creative process at every level is constituted by myriads of atomic events related in diverse ways. He calls these momentary events "actual entities" or "actual occasions." They vary unimaginably in complexity, and their forms of relatedness to one another differ immensely, too. Some, of utter simplicity, constitute so-called empty space. Others, in degrees of greater complexity, cluster in societies to constitute the atoms of minerals and plants and animal bodies, including our own. Still others, characterized by an extraordinarily rich balance of harmony and contrast, successively constitute the life of the human mind.

The differences of complexity and organization exhibited by these actual entities are simply staggering. Hence it is possible to draw a virtual infinity of distinctions in our analysis of them. But it is also the case that they have certain features in common: Each actual occasion, whether an ingredient of nature or of a human mind, is a synthesis of discrete impulses of "energy" or "feeling." Each is social, deriving that of which it is the synthesis from its past. The past determines the range of possibilities for each becoming occasion. In addition, the past "lures" each such entity to actualize certain possible syntheses rather than others. As a part of its given, each occasion also inherits from God a lure toward the ideal form of its becoming. But, ultimately—and here is the crucial point for our present consideration—each occasion in history and in nature is self-creative; how it constitutes itself cannot finally be explained without reference to its own self-directedness.

In Whitehead's view, then, those phenomena which contribute to the course of history have analogues, however remote, at every level of the natural process. And vice versa! The processes of nature have parallels in history. What occurs in the natural process *is* relevant to our estimate of human history. This is no less true for the wavering, uncertain, slow—but upward—process of evolutionary development; it, too, informs our understanding of the human potential.

Whitehead's account shows that neither as "nature" nor as "history" is the temporal process a fixed one, and that the potential for progress evident in the former must reside in the latter as well. Thus it provides for the possibility of historical progress. By itself, however, this Whiteheadian account of the temporal process fails to provide grounds for believing that there is any impetus toward the realization of the potential for progress in history. One could conclude that the advance of nature resulted by chance, or through forces no longer operable or at least not operable on the human level. Only if there is some agency which persistently seeks to translate the potential for the advance of freedom into a reality—only then is there a *justified* hope for the human future. For the Christian this agency is God.

Whitehead's account of the temporal process is thoroughly consistent with the Christian understanding of God as the lure toward freedom, developed and defended in Chapter Three on theological grounds. It enables a coherent affirmation of God as the supreme agent of freedom's growth, as the lure toward freedom present to each becoming actual entity at every level of reality in nature and in history.

The result of God's endeavor at the prehuman level is the evolutionary advance. Its circuitous, often tragic, climb reflects the risks of creativity. The path to every peak is threatened by fruitless diversion and loss; each success costs scores of failures. The achievement of no goal is assured. The preservation of no value is certain. Yet the divine labor continues. Its result to this point is the mighty creation of our world.

History may be viewed as the same divine endeavor qualified by the human level of response. The growth of freedom depends finally upon the faithfulness of God. Even so, God's relentless pursuit of freedom's advance mitigates neither the reality nor the importance of the human co-creatorship. Each human moment of becoming (like the becoming of every other actual occasion, to a lesser degree) is, in the final analysis, an instance of self-creation; it is informed and influenced, but not coerced, by its past. The purpose of God for the world, as that purpose is relevant to the occasion's specific potential for becoming, is one influence, one "cause," among others. It, like every other cause affecting the becoming occasion, is more or less efficacious, depending upon the receptivity of the creaturely response. It, like every other cause, is persuasive in power. The divine aim seeks to inspire, to lure; it does not, it cannot, coerce (see pp. 54–56 above). Thus divine action becomes ingredient in human action, without either being reduced to or displaced by the other.[76] History is the co-mingling of purposes human and divine. And to the degree that we on a given occasion conform to God's pursuit of freedom's advance, it is possible to say both: "We are working out our own salvation" *and* "God is at work in us" (cf. Phil. 2:12f.).

Our human response makes a genuine difference to the fate of God's aims for the world. If we choose to advance freedom at any level and in any place, the aims of God are advanced. If we hinder freedom we thwart the divine purpose. If we eventually destroy the human level of freedom, the subsequent temporal process could vacillate everlastingly at subordinate levels, or eventually a higher order might arise circumventing altogether humanity as we know it. No action is wholly self-contained. Every endeavor, human and divine, affects irrevocably what follows. Our present human action contributes to the enrichment or to the impoverishment of any future "heaven."

As freedom increases, the uncertainty of freedom's future multiplies. But this same increase also means that the divine aim is richer in potential and in the resources available for its achievement. Biblical experience witnesses to the divine ingenuity, the multifariousness of freedom's strategy under God. Sometimes freedom is posed for us as an open challenge: Choose you this day! Sometimes it is pitted against us unnoticed as we lounge numbly in the comforts of our captivity. Sometimes we are violently forced toward freedom. Such is the diversity of God's endeavor. As for the immediate consequence of that endeavor, it, too, varies immensely. There are a few occasions when it triumphs splendidly in full public view. There are more times when it works quietly in the memory of a faithful remnant. Not infrequently it languishes invisibly, sustained only in the dissatisfied suffering of the slave.[77]

The realism of biblical hope can scarcely be questioned. It is a hope fully appraised of sin's ingenuity, the creative deceit which freedom practices against itself. Biblical hope knows fully the depth of our prideful and slothful denials of freedom. But that same appraisal denies us the certitude of hopelessness. God is at work in the human world and we cannot be sure of the failure of this persuasive labor in and through us. We cannot be sure that the liberators will always be "involved in the same idolatries as the forces against which they contend."[78] We cannot be certain that every concrete success of freedom will always be matched by a new and comparable mode of bondage. We cannot be certain that the mixture of human motives must always be balanced toward self-seeking. We cannot be sure that human actions must always be dominated by the fearful disregard of freedom. In sum, however skeptical we may feel about freedom's prospect, the biblical witness keeps us skeptical of our skepticism. It refuses to deduce a vision of what can be from a reading of what has been and now is. It is not infatuated with the probable. It speaks, not of what is likely, but of what is possible. It believes, and it is justified in believing, in the potential for newness—new lives, new peoples, new heavens, and new earths. It can sustain this belief because it first of all believes in the persistent presence of a God "who by the power at work within us is able to do far more . . . than . . . we ask or think" (Eph. 3:20). To Christian faith, the basis of freedom's hope in history is the power of God in all reality.

THE NATURE OF FREEDOM'S FULFILLMENT

We have examined the place of freedom's fulfillment and the basis of Christian hope for the achievement of that future in every age. What, it might be asked in conclusion, about the nature of freedom's fulfillment? What will a redeemed freedom, richer and fuller, be like?

Insofar as such questioning seeks a description of fulfilled freedom, no final answer is possible, for two reasons. First, freedom is dynamic, ever retaining the capacity to surpass itself. Each fulfilling achievement introduces the potential for still other forms of enrichment. Our present "utopias," once achieved, would open to us visions of others now far beyond our dreams. The kingdom of God is a dynamic kingdom, as we have seen. No final description of it is possible because freedom has no fixed, final fulfillment.

No final answer to the question in this form is possible, secondly, because freedom is spontaneous as well as dynamic. Proximate fulfillments are genuine fulfillments; they are real embodiments of the kingdom of God, as liberation theologians have insisted. We can conceive of these "concrete utopias" and, as advocates of freedom, we must do so. Our pursuits of these utopias, however, are as much the creation of the artist as the construction of the engineer. To be sure, we may and must be doggedly empirical in our analyses of the forms of sin, the present structures of oppression. Our analysis of the way to liberation, too, must speak about the reality, social and political, of specific situations. But every path to freedom's fulfillment is, after all, freedom's path. And the element of creativity within freedom means that the fulfillment accomplished never fits precisely what had been predicted and pursued. The kingdom is open to our influence. It is subject to our contribution. But it is never bound by our anticipations or under our control.

Insofar as questioning about the nature of freedom's fulfillment seeks a chronology of freedom's journey, no answer at all is possible. Freedom has no timetable. Its history is not guaranteed. Thus a Christian language faithful to freedom eschews speculative chronologies of the future. It does not seek to discern the signs of the end time. "Of that day and hour," it says, "no one knows" (Mark 13:32). Its certitude is the God whose purpose and faithfulness are revealed in Jesus, the messiah of freedom. A Christian theology for freedom does not know of freedom's future. Believing in the God of freedom, it knows of freedom's worth. Thus, unequivocally, it calls us to the service of every freedom everywhere.

Notes

1. Norman Perrin, *Rediscovering the Teaching of Jesus* (New York: Harper & Row, 1967), p. 67.

2. Ibid., p. 164; cf. pp. 159–64.

3. Robert W. Funk, "Apocalyptic as a Historical and Theological Problem in Current New Testament Scholarship," in Robert W. Funk, ed., *Apocalypticism*, Journal for Theology and Church, Vol. 6 (New York: Herder and Herder, 1969), p. 182.

4. Funk, in ibid., p. 183. Ernst Käsemann shares this view (see his "On the Topic of Primitive Christian Apocalyptic," in ibid., p. 104), as does Hans Conzelmann (see "Present and Future in the Synoptic Tradition," in Robert W. Funk and

Gerhard Ebeling, eds., *God and Christ: Existence and Province,* Journal for Theology and Church, Vol. 5 [New York: Harper & Row, 1968], pp. 26–44).

5. Perrin, *Rediscovering the Teaching of Jesus,* p. 56.

6. See Hans Dieter Betz, "On the Problem of the Religio-Historical Understanding of Apocalypticism," in R. W. Funk, ed., *Apocalypticism,* pp. 134–38.

7. For a fuller description, see Frank M. Cross, "New Directions in the Study of Apocalyptic," in ibid., pp. 157ff.

8. See the debate of Käsemann, Gerhard Ebeling, and Ernst Fuchs in the first four essays in ibid., pp. 17–133.

9. David Noel Freedman, "The Flowering of Apocalyptic," in ibid., p. 167.

10. On this see Funk, in ibid., pp. 185–89.

11. This judgment is explicit in Funk's analysis (ibid., p. 183) and in Käsemann's (ibid., p. 40).

12. Norman Cohn, *The Pursuit of the Millennium* (New York: Harper & Row, 1961), p. 13.

13. For a description of this development, see Peter Muller-Goldkuhle, "Post-Biblical Developments in Eschatological Thought," in E. Schillebeeckx, O. P., and B. Willems, O. P., eds., *The Problem of Eschatology,* Concilium 41 (New York: Paulist Press, 1969), pp. 24–41.

14. See Johannes Weiss, *Die Predigt Jesu vom Reiche Gottes* (1892) and Albert Schweitzer, *The Quest of the Historical Jesus* (1906).

15. Karl Barth, *The Epistle to the Romans* (London: Oxford University Press, 1933), p. 314.

16. Ibid., p. 402.

17. Rubem Alves offers a sustained analysis of Barth on this point in *A Theology of Human Hope* (St. Meinrad, Ind.: Abbey Press, 1974), pp. 44–55.

18. Rudolph Bultmann, *Kerygma and Myth* (New York: Harper & Row, 1961), pp. 319f.

19. Ibid., p. 19. For criticism of Bultmann's existential interpretation of eschatology, see Rubem Alves, *A Theology of Human Hope,* pp. 34–43; Jürgen Moltmann, *The Theology of Hope* (New York: Harper & Row, 1967), esp., pp. 65–69, and Dorothee Soelle, *Political Theology* (Philadelphia: Fortress Press, 1974).

20. In addition to Moltmann's work (see previous note) the reader should see Johannes B. Metz, *Theology of the World* (New York: Herder and Herder, 1971), and Wolfhart Pannenberg, *Theology and the Kingdom of God* (Philadelphia: Westminster Press, 1969), for literature representative of this development in its earlier stages.

21. Moltmann, *Theology of Hope,* p. 16; cf. pp. 108ff.

22. Ibid., p. 109.

23. Ibid., p. 85.

24. Ibid., p. 21; cf. p. 329.

25. Ibid., p. 179; cf. pp. 165–202 and his *Religion, Revolution and the Future* (New York: Scribner's, 1969).

26. Moltmann, *Theology of Hope,* p. 86; cf. p. 148.

27. Ibid., pp. 87f.

28. Ibid., pp. 88, 178–81, 216–29.

29. Ibid., p. 221. Cf., too, Moltmann's *The Church in the Power of the Spirit* (New York: Harper & Row, 1977), pp. 189–96.

30. Ibid., p. 16.

31. Juan Luis Segundo, S.J., *The Liberation of Theology* (Maryknoll, N.Y.: Orbis Books, 1976), p. 144. Segundo's statement is made about "German 'political theology' " in general, but it is related specifically to Moltmann, Rudolf Weth, and Johannes Metz. Moltmann accepts this as a description of his view, and responds to Segundo's criticism in "On Latin American Liberation Theology," *Christianity and Crisis* 36 (March 29, 1976): 58.

32. On this see Gustavo Gutiérrez, *Theology of Liberation* (Maryknoll, N.Y.: Orbis Books, 1973), pp. 53–77, and Juan Luis Segundo, *Liberation of Theology*, pp. 139–42.

33. See Segundo, *Liberation of Theology*, pp. 142–44.

34. Cited in Reinhold Niebuhr, *The Nature and Destiny of Man* (New York: Scribner's, 1955), Vol. II, p. 194.

35. Quoted in Segundo, *Liberation of Theology*, p. 143.

36. Literature introducing liberation theology is cited in Chapter Three, note 12. Robert McAfee Brown's *Theology in a New Key*, cited there, provides, too, thorough reference to critiques of liberation theology (see ch. 4). For a more recent critique, see Edward R. Norman, *Christianity and the World Order* (New York: Oxford University Press, 1979). Responses to Norman's charges have appeared in *Christianity and Crisis* 39 (March 19, 1979) and subsequent issues.

37. Gutiérrez, *Theology of Liberation*, pp. 152f.; see pp. 149–87 for a full statement of Gutiérrez' view.

38. Leonardo Boff, "Salvation in Jesus Christ and the Process of Liberation," in Claude Geffré and Gustavo Gutiérrez, eds., *The Mystical and Political Dimension of the Christian Faith*, Concilium 96 (New York: Herder and Herder, 1974), p. 81. Cf. Boff, *Jesus Christ Liberator* (Maryknoll, N.Y.: Orbis Books, 1978), ch. 3 and passim; Jon Sobrino, *Christology at the Crossroads* (Maryknoll, N.Y.: Orbis Books, 1978), pp. xxv, 119, 230, and Gutiérrez, *Theology of Liberation*, pp. 167f.

39. Boff, in Geffré and Gutiérrez, eds., *Mystical and Political Dimensions*, p. 80.

40. Rubem A. Alves, "Christian Realism: Ideology of the Establishment," *Christianity and Crisis* 33 (September 17, 1973): 175. See the exchange between Thomas G. Sanders and Rubem Alves in this issue, pp. 167–76, and the continuation of the discussion by others in the October 15, 1973, issue, pp. 196–206.

41. Gutiérrez, *Theology of Liberation*, p. 238.

42. Ibid., pp. 235, 177.

43. Ibid., pp. 176f. and ch. 2.

44. Although Gutiérrez uses "denunciation" and "annunciation" to designate the dual functions of utopianism at the second level of liberation (see *Theology of Liberation*, pp. 232–39), these terms also accurately describe the two functions of the inclusive process of liberation.

45. Juan Luis Segundo, "Capitalism—Socialism: A Theological Crux," in Geffré and Gutiérrez, eds., *Mystical and Political Dimensions*, p. 121.

46. See, e.g., Raúl Vidales, "Some Recent Publications in Latin America on the Theology of Liberation," in ibid., p. 129, and Gutiérrez, *Theology of Liberation*, p. 168.

47. Segundo, in Geffré and Gutiérrez, eds., *Mystical and Political Dimensions*, p. 115.

48. Johannes Metz is especially susceptible to this interpretation. He suggests that Christian "social teaching" is primarily "social criticism" based on the "eschatological proviso" which reveals *all* social achievements to be provisional (see,

e.g., *Theology of the World*, pp. 114, 131ff., 151ff.). Segundo discusses the consequences of, and rejects, this position in *Liberation of Theology*, pp. 144f., and in Geffré and Gutiérrez, eds., *Mystical and Political Dimensions*, pp. 110ff. A similar response to recent European theology is found in Hugo Assmann, *Theology for a Nomad Church* (Maryknoll, N.Y.: Orbis Books, 1976), pp. 92–96.

49. Segundo, in Geffré and Gutiérrez, eds., *Mystical and Political Dimensions*, pp. 116f.

50. Ibid., pp. 120f.

51. Boff, in ibid., p. 85.

52. Enrique Dussel, "Domination—Liberation: A New Approach," in ibid., p. 46. Gutiérrez writes in the same vein; see, e.g., *Theology of Liberation*, pp. 155–79.

53. See J. N. D. Kelly, *Early Christian Doctrines* (New York: Harper, 1958), pp. 223–237.

54. Ibid., p. 340; see pp. 310–43.

55. Boff, in Geffré and Gutiérrez, eds., *Mystical and Political Dimensions*, p. 84.

56. Segundo, *Liberation of Theology*, p. 150 (italics removed).

57. Segundo, "Capitalism—Socialism," in Geffré and Gutiérrez, eds., *Mystical and Political Dimensions*, p. 123. Moltmann says this view is more Pelagian than that of Pelagius, in "On Latin American Liberation Theology," *Christianity and Crisis* 36 (March 29, 1976): 58.

58. Segundo, *Liberation of Theology*, p. 150 (italics removed).

59. Gutiérrez, *Theology of Liberation*, pp. 173, 155–57.

60. For the balancing element in Segundo and Gutiérrez, see, respectively, "Capitalism—Socialism" in Geffré and Gutiérrez, eds., *Mystical and Political Dimensions*, p. 123, and *Theology of Liberation*, p. 159.

61. Alves, *Theology of Human Hope*, p. 144.

62. Ibid., p. 116.

63. Ibid., p. 143. The first quotation is from Maurice S. Friedman, *Martin Buber: The Life of Dialogue* (Chicago: University of Chicago Press, 1956), p. 252. The biblical source is Philippians 2:12f.

64. This point has here been substantiated exclusively by reference to Latin American theologies of liberation. In the broad sense of the term, "liberation theology" may also refer to the exceedingly important work of others (e.g., black theologians such as James Cone and J. Deotis Roberts, feminist theologians such as Rosemary Ruether and Letty M. Russell, and North American white males such as Frederick Herzog). We have focused upon Latin American liberation theology primarily because it is more widely and systematically developed and thus more readily illustrative of the point being made.

65. Gutiérrez, *Theology of Liberation*, p. 13.

66. Ibid., p. 153. See, too, the completion of the sentence cited in the previous note.

67. Moltmann, *Theology of Hope*, pp. 105f. (italics added).

68. Alfredo Fierro, *The Militant Gospel* (New York: Orbis Books, 1975), p. 284.

69. Alfred North Whitehead, *Process and Reality* (New York: Macmillan Company, 1929), p. 394.

70. Ibid., p. 392.

71. Some of the material in this section is adapted from the more detailed discussion appearing in my article, "Hope for the Human Future: Niebuhr, Whitehead and Utopian Expectation," *The Iliff Review* 32 (Fall 1975): 3–18.

72. Reinhold Niebuhr, *The Nature and Destiny of Man* (New York: Scribner's, 1944), Vol. II, p. 85.

73. Reinhold Niebuhr, *Faith and History* (New York: Scribner's, 1949), p. 227.

74. See Gutiérrez, *Theology of Liberation*, pp. 149–60.

75. Niebuhr, *Faith and History*, p. 66.

76. For a Whiteheadian account of the relationship of divine and human action, see David R. Griffin, *A Process Christology* (Philadelphia: Westminster Press, 1973), ch. 3, esp. pp. 92ff.

77. See the discussion of this point in Rubem Alves, *Tomorrow's Child* (New York: Harper & Row, 1972), ch. 8 (esp. pp. 131–39), and in *A Theology of Human Hope*, pp. 114–22, 151.

78. Niebuhr, *Faith and History*, p. 227.

Index

Compiled by William E. Jerman, ASI

Actual entity (Whitehead), 30
Agape, 49-52
Alves, Rubem, 33, 116, 119-20
Annunciation (and Denunciation), 118, 131
Anxiety, 64-66, 101-2, 104
Apocolypticism, 109-13, 121
Aquinas, Thomas, 11
Arendt, Hanna, 6
Aristotle, 11
Arius, 119
Arrogance, 68-69
Aseity, divine, 8, 47-52, 63
Athanasius, St., 76
Augustine, St., 11, 15-16, 70, 76-78, 81

Baier, Kurt, 45
Barnes, Hazel, 27
Barth, Karl, 48, 49, 52, 57, 113
Beardslee, William A., 89
Blake, William, 14
Bloch, Ernst, 47
Boff, Leonardo, 116
Bondage, 81, 99-101
Bultmann, Rudolf, 20, 79, 113

Christology, 88-105, 118-19
Cohn, Norman, 112
Community, 54
Consciousness, 22-25, 28
Condorcet, Marquis de, 13
Cosmic order, reason, 5-7, 12
Creativity, 31-33, 37, 54, 72
Cross, 99, 101-2

Death, 82-84, 101-2
Descartes, René, 13, 28
Doty, William G., 89

Dualism(s), 115-16, 125-26
Dussel, Enrique, 118

Ego, 22-23
Engels, Friedrich, 25
Enlightenment, 13, 15
Eros, 49
Eschatology, 108-129
Euripedes, 5
Evaluation, 29, 53-54, 58
Existentialism, 22-24
Ex nihilo, 8, 22, 24, 25, 47, 114-15
Exousia, 97

Fate, 6
Fierro, Alfredo, 123
Foreknowledge, divine, 45-46, 58-59
Forsakenness, 101
Freedom: as an Abstraction, 9, 15, 34, 52; as Autonomy, 4; as Consciousness, 23; and Context, 31, 33-36, 51, 67-70, 77; and Creativity, 4, 9, 15, 22-23, 31-36, 77, 119; Denial of, 43-46, 56, 80, 83; Elements of, 31-36; Fulfillment of, 59, 123-29; and Law, 9; as Liberation, 92-93, 98; as Negative, 32; as Obligation, 93-96, 98; as Political freedom, 7; as Responsibility, 96-98; as Spontaneity, 4, 31-32; and Transcendence, 71; and Value, 34-35, 53-54
Freire, Paulo, 33, 66
Friedman, Maurice S., 120
Funk, Robert W., 89, 108-9
Future, 58, 108

Garaudy, Roger, 28, 43-44, 47

135

God: Autonomy of, 8; Christian under-
 standing of, 43-44, 52, 55-56, 127; as
 Creator, 8-9, 15; Dependence of,
 50-51; Freedom of, 51-57, 104; as
 Love, 48, 54; Omniscient, 55, 59;
 and Power, 54-56, 58-59; Will of,
 8-10
Goethe, Johann Wolfgang, 16-17
González Ruiz, José María, 45
Good, true, beautiful, 6-8, 14
Greek influence, 4-8, 15, 112
Gutiérrez, Gustavo, 116-17, 119

Habit, 77-78
Hebraic influence, 7-10, 15
Hebrews, Epistle to, 99
Hegel, Georg W.F., 16, 47
Hesiod, 6
History, 121-22, 124-25, 127
Hodgson, Peter, 73, 89-92, 97
Homer, 5-6
Hope, 112, 114, 121-22, 124, 128
Husserl, Edmund, 23

Ignorance, 6
Ingratitude, 67-68
Injustice, 69, 79-81
Intuition, 5-6, 10, 15

Jaspers, Karl, 3
Jeremias, Joachim, 101
Jesus Christ: Authority claimed by,
 96-98; and Gospel of freedom,
 89-90, 92, 94-95, 101; and Law,
 90-91; and Women, 91-92
Job, Book of, 10
John, Gospel of, 50, 91, 111
Justice, socio-political, 69, 95

Kant, Immanuel, 13-14
Käsemann, Ernst, 88, 90
Keats, John, 13
Kierkegaard, Søren, 17-18, 65, 88
Kingdom of God, 88-89, 92-93, 108-10,
 114-21, 123-24, 129

Law, 90-95
Legalism, 9-11

Liberation theology, 47, 108, 115-17,
 119-21, 125, 129, 132
Love, 49, 53
Luke-Acts, 99, 111
Luke, Gospel of, 89, 91, 94
Luther, Martin, 115

Mann, Thomas, 14
Marcuse, Herbert, 72
Mark, Gospel of, 71, 89-90, 92, 95-96,
 99
Marx, Karl, 27
Marxism, 24-28, 33
Marxsen, Willi, 93
Materialism, 25, 27-28
Matthew, Gospel of, 90, 92-93, 97-99,
 104
Messiah, 110
Metz, Johannes, 114, 131
Mirandola, Pico della, 16
Moira, 6, 10
Moltmann, Jürgen, 114-15, 122
Monotheism, 47
Morality, 6
Muller, Herbert J., 7
Müller, Ronald, 81

"Naming the animals" (Adam), 9, 15,
 19, 35, 53
Nature, 82
Nature, human, mirror of divine, 8-9,
 15, 44, 53, 56
Need, 25-27, 29
Neoplatonism, 10-11
Niebuhr, Reinhold, 65-67, 70, 104,
 124-25
Nietzsche, Friedrich, 17-18, 21, 29,
 34-35
Nihilism, 17-18
Non-historical, 122
Nonhuman, 56
Nothingness, 23-24

Obedience, 9, 45, 69
Oppression, 66, 70, 129
Origen, 112
Original sin, 75-82

Pannenberg, Wolfhart, 43, 46, 114
Parables (biblical), 89-91, 94, 118
Parousia, 113
Paul, St., 69, 73-79, 82-84, 99-100, 102, 104
Perrin, Norman, 89, 92, 108
Plato, 5-6, 55
Political theology, 116-17
Pride, 66-67, 72, 74, 85, 102
Process philosophy, 34, 37, 103
Project (Sartre), 24-26
Proposition (Whitehead), 123-24

Rationalism, 12, 14
Reason, 5-7, 11, 15
Rebellion against God, 10
Reductionism, 25-26
Resurrection, 102-5, 114
Romanticism, 13-16
Rubenstein, Richard, 9

Salvation, 120, 123
Sartre, Jean-Paul, 21-29, 33, 34, 66, 74
Schweitzer, Albert, 113
Secular, 9, 21
Segundo, Juan Luis, 117-19
Self (selfhood), 5-7, 10, 12, 14-15, 18, 22, 65
Self-deception, 73-75
Sensuality, 66, 70-73, 85, 102
Sexuality, 85

Sin, 6, 64-84, 129; Objectification of, 76-82
Social efficiency, 72
Social structures, 23-24, 30, 79, 126
Socialism, 117-18
Socrates, 6-7
Sophocles, 7
Spontaneity, 4, 23, 31-32, 129
Stoicism, 7, 10
Synoptic Gospels, 93, 110

Tertullian, 70, 76
Theology, Christian, 8, 44-45, 47
Third World, 85

Unfreedom, 100
Utopianism, 116-17

Value(s), 29, 34, 53-54
Victorianism, 14
Virgil, 11
Volition, 11, 14-15

Warren, Robert Penn, 74-75
Weiss, Johannes, 113
Weth, Rudolf, 116
Whitehead, Alfred North, 21, 28-31, 53, 55, 121, 126-27
Wordsworth, William, 13
World, 23

Other Orbis books . . .

THE MEANING OF MISSION

José Comblin

"This very readable book has made me think, and I feel it will be useful for anyone dealing with their Christian role of mission and evangelism." *New Review of Books and Religion*

ISBN 0-88344-304-X CIP   *Cloth $6.95*

THE GOSPEL OF PEACE AND JUSTICE

Catholic Social Teaching Since Pope John

Presented by Joseph Gremillion

"Especially valuable as a resource. The book brings together 22 documents containing the developing social teaching of the church from *Mater et Magistra* to Pope Paul's 1975 *Peace Day Message on Reconciliation*. I watched the intellectual excitement of students who used Gremillion's book in a justice and peace course I taught last summer, as they discovered a body of teaching on the issues they had defined as relevant. To read Gremillion's overview and prospectus, a meaty introductory essay of some 140 pages, is to be guided through the sea of social teaching by a remarkably adept navigator."

National Catholic Reporter

"An authoritative guide and study aid for concerned Catholics and others." *Library Journal*

ISBN 0-88344-165-9   *Cloth $15.95*
ISBN 0-88344-166-7   *Paper $8.95*

THEOLOGY IN THE AMERICAS

Papers of the 1975 Detroit Conference

Edited by Sergio Torres and John Eagleson

"A pathbreaking book from and about a pathbreaking theological conference, *Theology in the Americas* makes a major contribution to ecumenical theology, Christian social ethics and liberation movements in dialogue." *Fellowship*

ISBN 0-88344-479-8 CIP   *Cloth $12.95*
ISBN 0-88344-476-3   *Paper $5.95*

MARX AND THE BIBLE

José Miranda

"An inescapable book which raises more questions than it answers, which will satisfy few of us, but will not let us rest easily again. It is an attempt to utilize the best tradition of Scripture scholarship to understand the text when it is set in a context of human need and misery."

Walter Brueggemann, in Interpretation
ISBN 0-88344-306-6   *Cloth $8.95*
ISBN 0-88344-307-4   *Paper $4.95*

BEING AND THE MESSIAH

The Message of Saint John

José Miranda

"This book could become the catalyst of a new debate on the Fourth Gospel. Johannine scholarship will hotly debate the 'terrifyingly revolutionary thesis that this world of contempt and oppression can be changed into a world of complete selflessness and unrestricted mutual assistance.' Cast in the framework of an analysis of contemporary philosophy, the volume will prove a classic of Latin American theology." *Frederick Herzog, Duke University Divinity School*

ISBN 0-88344-027-X CIP   *Cloth $8.95*
ISBN 0-88344-028-8   *Paper $4.95*

THE GOSPEL IN SOLENTINAME

Ernesto Cardenal

"Upon reading this book, I want to do so many things—burn all my other books which at best seem like hay, soggy with mildew. I now know who (not what) is the church and how to celebrate church in the eucharist. The dialogues are intense, profound, radical. *The Gospel in Solentiname* calls us home."

Carroll Stuhlmueller, National Catholic Reporter
ISBN 0-88344-168-3   *Vol. 1 Cloth $6.95*
ISBN 0-88344-170-5   *Vol. 1 Paper $4.95*
ISBN 0-88344-167-5   *Vol. 2 Cloth $6.95*

THEOLOGY FOR A NOMAD CHURCH

Hugo Assmann

"A new challenge to contemporary theology which attempts to show that the theology of liberation is not just a fad, but a new political dimension which touches every aspect of Christian existence."

Publishers Weekly

ISBN 0-88344-493-3   *Cloth $7.95*
ISBN 0-88344-494-1   *Paper $4.95*

FREEDOM MADE FLESH
The Mission of Christ and His Church

Ignacio Ellacuría

"Ellacuría's main thesis is that God's saving message and revelation are historical, that is, that the proclamation of the gospel message must possess the same historical character that revelation and salvation history do and that, for this reason, it must be carried out in history and in a historical way." *Cross and Crown*

ISBN 0-88344-140-3   *Cloth $8.95*
ISBN 0-88344-141-1   *Paper $4.95*

THE LIBERATION OF THEOLOGY

Juan Luis Segundo

"It is a remarkable book in terms of its boldness in confronting the shortcomings of the Christian tradition and in terms of the clarity of vision provided by the hermeneutic of liberation. Segundo writes with ease whether dealing with the sociological, theological, or political roots of liberation. His is a significant addition to the recent work of Cone, Alves, Moltmann, and Gutiérrez because it compels the movement to interrogate its own theological foundations. A necessary addition, in one of the more fruitful directions of contemporary theology, it is appropriate for graduate, undergraduate, or clerical readers." *Choice*

"The book makes for exciting reading and should not be missing in any theological library." *Library Journal*

ISBN 0-88344-285-X CIP   *Cloth $10.95*
ISBN 0-88344-286-8   *Paper $6.95*

THE CHURCH AND POWER IN BRAZIL

Charles Antoine

"This is a book which should serve as a basis of discussion and further study by all who are interested in the relationship of the Church to contemporary governments, and all who believe that the Church has a vital role to play in the quest for social justice." *Worldmission*
ISBN 0-88344-062-8   *Paper $4.95*

HISTORY AND
THE THEOLOGY OF LIBERATION

Enrique Dussel

"The book is easy reading. It is a brilliant study of what may well be or should be the future course of theological methodology."
Religious Media Today
ISBN 0-88344-179-9   *Cloth $8.95*
ISBN 0-88344-180-2   *Paper $4.95*

DOM HELDER CAMARA

José de Broucker

"De Broucker, an internationally recognized journalist, develops a portrait, at once intimate, comprehensive and sympathetic, of the Archbishop of Olinda and Recife, Brazil, whose championship of political and economic justice for the hungry, unorganized masses of his country and all Latin America has aroused world attention."
America
ISBN 0-88344-099-7   *Cloth $6.95*

THE DESERT IS FERTILE

Dom Helder Camara

"Camara's brief essays and poems are arresting for their simplicity and depth of vision, and are encouraging because of the realistic yet quietly hopeful tone with which they argue for sustained action toward global justice." *Commonweal*
ISBN 0-88344-078-4   *Cloth $3.95*